T0328674

Cambridge Elements ≡

Elements in Metaphysics
edited by
Tuomas E. Tahko
University of Bristol

INDETERMINACY
IN THE WORLD

Alessandro Torza
National Autonomous University of Mexico

CAMBRIDGE
UNIVERSITY PRESS

Shaftesbury Road, Cambridge CB2 8EA, United Kingdom

One Liberty Plaza, 20th Floor, New York, NY 10006, USA

477 Williamstown Road, Port Melbourne, VIC 3207, Australia

314–321, 3rd Floor, Plot 3, Splendor Forum, Jasola District Centre, New Delhi – 110025, India

103 Penang Road, #05–06/07, Visioncrest Commercial, Singapore 238467

Cambridge University Press is part of Cambridge University Press & Assessment, a department of the University of Cambridge.

We share the University's mission to contribute to society through the pursuit of education, learning and research at the highest international levels of excellence.

www.cambridge.org
Information on this title: www.cambridge.org/9781009056014

DOI: 10.1017/9781009057370

First published April 2023

A catalogue record for this publication is available from the British Library.

ISBN 978-1-009-05601-4 Paperback
ISSN 2633-9862 (online)
ISSN 2633-9854 (print)

Indeterminacy in the World

Elements in Metaphysics

DOI: 10.1017/9781009057370
First published online: April 2023

Alessandro Torza
National Autonomous University of Mexico
Author for correspondence: Alessandro Torza, atorza@me.com

Abstract: The way we represent the world in thought and language is shot through with indeterminacy: we speak of red apples and yellow apples without thereby committing to any sharp cutoff between the application of the predicate 'red' and of the predicate 'yellow'. But can reality itself be indeterminate? In other words, can indeterminacy originate in the mind-independent world, and not only in our representations? If so, can the phenomenon also arise at the microscopic scale of fundamental physics? Section 1 of this Element provides a brief overview of the question of indeterminacy. Section 2 discusses the thesis that the world is comprised of indeterminate objects, whereas Section 3 focuses on the thesis that there are indeterminate states of affairs. Finally, Section 4 is devoted to the case study of indeterminacy in quantum physics.

Keywords: metaphysical indeterminacy, truthmaker semantics, quantum logic, bivalence, vagueness

ISBNs: 9781009056014 (PB), 9781009057370 (OC)
ISSNs: 2633-9862 (online), 2633-9854 (print)

Contents

1 Introduction

There is a difference between a shaky and out-of-focus photograph and a snapshot of clouds and fog banks.

Erwin Schrödinger

1.1 Scope

This Element is about indeterminacy insofar as it does not originate in the way we represent the world in mind or language. Following tradition, I will be referring to such a phenomenon as *metaphysical* or *worldly indeterminacy*. Here is a preliminary gloss on indeterminacy as such:

It is indeterminate whether p if, and only if (iff) there is no fact of the matter whether p.

The gloss provides us with a way of classifying indeterminacy based on its source. When there is no fact of the matter whether p because there is no fact of the matter about the meaning of 'p', we speak of *semantic* or *linguistic indeterminacy*. When there is no fact of the matter whether p despite there being a fact of the matter about the meaning of 'p', we speak of metaphysical indeterminacy (Section 3.1).

Indeterminacy ought not be confused with *indefiniteness* in the following sense: a declarative sentence 'p' is indefinite iff it is not truth-evaluable. Because indeterminacy whether p presupposes that 'p' is truth-evaluable, indefiniteness and indeterminacy are incompatible.

Indeterminacy must also be distinguished from *vagueness*, the phenomenon arising in the presence of a sorites series. If we line up all persons in the world ordered by the number (or density) of hairs on their head, starting from those who are completely hairless all the way to the most hirsute, there is no single step in the series that we can confidently mark as a cutoff between bald and nonbald people. This phenomenon famously leads to paradox (assuming classical logic). One standard solution to vagueness-related phenomena appeals to indeterminacy. Accordingly, the reason we are unable to identify a sharp cutoff between bald and nonbald people is that there is none: some people are such that there is no fact of the matter whether they are bald. Because indeterminacy has been studied mostly in relation to vagueness, the two phenomena are often terminologically conflated. This Element is squarely focused on indeterminacy in its own right.

In order to get a preliminary grasp of indeterminacy and neighboring notions, as well as on the possible sources of indeterminacy, consider the following statements:

1. Vulcan has no determinate mass.
2. It is indeterminate whether the present king of France weighs more than 80 kg.

3. It is indeterminate whether Woody Harrelson is bald.
4. It is indeterminate whether the cardinality of the continuum is the least uncountable cardinal.
5. 'This sentence is false' has no determinate truth value.
6. It is indeterminate whether there will be a sea battle tomorrow.
7. Electrons with determinate momentum have indeterminate position.

Each of these claims is prima facie true. Sentence 1 appears to be true insofar as 'Vulcan' is a name that nineteenth-century astronomer Urbain Le Verrier introduced in order to designate a hypothetical planet, which eventually turned out not to exist. Sentence 2 also rings true insofar as France is not a kingdom. Sentence 3 is a plausible consequence of the fact that Woody Harrelson has lost much, though not all, of his hair. Sentence 4 aims to capture the mathematical fact that the standard axiomatization of set theory does not settle the identities of transfinite cardinals in all cases. Sentence 5 is a way to articulate the liar paradox, a classical antinomy of self-reference. Sentence 6 aims to capture the idea that the future is open insofar as the present does not settle which events will eventually take place. Finally, sentence 7 conveys the fact that the properties of position and momentum of a quantum system are complementary, in the sense that they cannot both have determinate values at the same time.

Each of sentences 1–8 contains the word '(in)determinate'. Do they all express instances of indeterminacy, as the wording seems to imply? Also, do all instances of indeterminacy have the same source? The answer to both questions is, arguably, no.

In order to address the first question, we need a better characterization of indeterminacy as such. Since our main focus is indeterminacy so long as it originates in the nonrepresentational world, we can remain agnostic about the answer to the more general question. For present purpose, I defer to the proposal articulated in (Taylor, 2018: 20), that roughly goes like so:

It is indeterminate whether p just in case there is a type of fact whose job is to settle the truth value of 'p', yet fails to settle the truth value of 'p'.

It immediately follows that, despite appearances, 1 and 2 are not true. Because 'Vulcan' is an empty name, there are no facts that could settle the truth value of statements in which that name occurs. So the term 'determinate' is a red herring. Similar considerations apply to 2 insofar as the term 'the present King of France' is irreferential. Due to a lack of facts of the relevant type, statements 1 and 2 are best categorized as cases of indefiniteness rather than indeterminacy.

Sentence 3, on the other hand, is a prototypical case of indeterminacy. Indeed, the number (or density) of hairs on Woody Harrelson's head is the type of fact that could make 'Woody Harrelson is bald' either true or false. But although Woody Harrelson has been going bald, he is not quite there yet. So the relevant fact fails to settle the truth value of 'Woody Harrelson is bald'.

Whether 4 expresses a bona fide instance of indeterminacy cannot be settled without saying more about the set-theoretic universe (cf. Scambler, 2020). We will return to this point in Section 2.1.

It is also an open question whether 5 expresses an instance of indeterminacy because it is unclear which facts, if any, could settle the truth value of 'This sentence is false'. Were it to turn out that there are no such facts, 5 would then be another instance of indefiniteness (cf. Barker, 2014; Newhard, 2020).

Statement 6 concerns the problem of the open future, which goes back to *De Interpretatione* (Aristotle, 1963: 18 b 23). The kind of fact whose job is to settle the present truth value of 'There will be a sea battle tomorrow' is the present state of the world. But insofar as there may or may not be a sea battle tomorrow given the way the world presently is, Taylor's characterization guarantees that 6, as well as any other future contingent, expresses an instance of indeterminacy (cf. Thomason, 1970; Barnes & Cameron, 2008; Mariani & Torrengo, 2021).

Finally, sentence 7 also appears to be a case of indeterminacy, since we know what type of facts could settle the truth value of a sentence ascribing such and such momentum to a system of electrons, namely facts about which state the system is in. And whenever the state – which can be specified with outmost precision – allows us to ascribe a particular position value, it will also prevent us from ascribing any determinate momentum value. The topic of quantum indeterminacy is discussed at length in Section 4.

In conclusion, these examples contain three plausible candidates for indeterminacy (3, 6, 7), as well as two tentative candidates (4, 5).

On to the second question. We had set out to establish whether all instances of indeterminacy have the same source. When it comes to 3, the standard diagnosis of why the facts about Woody Harrelson's hair underdetermine the truth value of 'Woody Harrelson is bald' is that the predicate 'bald' has no precise extension. On the other hand, the indeterminacy expressed in 6 does not originate in any linguistic imprecision. If it is indeed indeterminate whether there is going to be a sea battle tomorrow, that is due to the way the world is rather than the semantics of 'battle' or 'tomorrow'. Likewise with 7: if there is indeterminacy at the microscopic scale, it is due not to imprecision in the language of quantum mechanics, but to the structure of quantum systems themselves (Section 4.4). Therefore, whereas 3 appears to express an instance of semantic indeterminacy, 6 and 7 arguably express cases of indeterminacy that is worldly in character. Scenarios like the ones described in 6 and 7 (and perhaps 4 and 5) are the subject of the present Element.

1.2 Background

Until not long ago, the subject of metaphysical indeterminacy used to be taboo. Russell (1923: 85) famously claimed that "apart from representation, whether cognitive or mechanical, there can be such thing as vagueness or precision: things are what they are." In the same vein, Lewis (1986: 212) wrote:

> [T]he only intelligible account of vagueness locates it in our thought and language. The reason it is vague where the outback begins is not that there's this thing, the outback, with imprecise borders; rather there are many things, with different borders, and nobody has been fool enough to try to enforce a choice of one of them as the official referent of the word "outback."

The idea that indeterminacy cannot arise in the nonrepresentational world is also voiced in Dummett (1975: 314), Evans (1978), and Heller (1996).

The past couple of decades have seen a vigorous reaction to the received view, however, with the bulk of the effort going into showing that we can at least coherently theorize about metaphysical indeterminacy. This thesis is going to be the topic of Sections 2 and 3. The former discusses the view that there can be indeterminate objects, whereas the latter is devoted to the (more promising) view that indeterminacy arises at the level of states of affairs. A further issue is whether metaphysical indeterminacy is not merely possible, but actual. Section 4 answers in the affirmative by arguing that metaphysical indeterminacy arises at the scale of atomic and subatomic particles.

People who theorize about and acknowledge the existence of indeterminacy fall under one of two categories: monists, who take indeterminacy to be either all semantic or all metaphysical in character (Keefe, 2000; Eklund, 2008; Akiba, 2014b); and pluralists, who allow for indeterminacy of either kind (Williams, 2008b; Torza, 2022). The default view throughout the twentieth century was semantic monism. However, it is now not unusual to find pluralists, as well as a handful of metaphysical monists.

Throughout the discussions, it will be assumed that the notion of metaphysical indeterminacy, if coherent, is not disjunctive. For all we know, the assumption may be misguided and the instances of indeterminacy in the world structurally too dissimilar. In the absence of evidence to the contrary, however, I will stick to the working hypothesis that the notion of metaphysical indeterminacy is nondisjunctive, for the sake of both ideological parsimony and theoretical unification.

Besides the aforementioned cases of indeterminacy, such as set theory, quantum mechanics, and the open future, there are other putative instances that, for reason of space, will not be covered. A nonexhaustive list includes indeterminacy about chances (Bradley, 2016), morality (Schoenfield, 2016), existence (Barnes, 2013; Loss, 2018 Sud, forthcoming.), naturalness (Torza, 2020b), and causation (Bernstein, 2016), as well as the laws of physics (Chen, 2022) and metaphysics (Wasserman, 2017).

2 Objects

2.1 Identity, Parthood, Location

What would it take for the world to display indeterminacy? On one popular view, the world is the totality of objects (Quine, 1948; Boolos, 1984; Rayo & Yablo, 2001). If so, for the world to be indeterminate is for it to contain indeterminate objects. This ontic perspective is going to be the guiding idea of Section 2.

Taken at face value, the idea may seem like a nonstarter since indeterminacy talk typically occurs in expressions such as 'it is determinate that' and 'it is indeterminate whether', which apply to sentences, not names. So the linguistic evidence suggests that determinacy and lack thereof are, if anything, properties of propositions, or states of affairs, and that predicating (in)determinacy of objects is a category mistake.

It is nevertheless possible to massage object indeterminacy into something intelligible. Let '$\mathbf{D}p$' stand for 'it is determinate that p', and '∇p' for 'it is indeterminate whether p', which can be unpacked as '$\neg \mathbf{D}p \wedge \neg \mathbf{D}\neg p$'. Insofar as being an object is to be something, here is a natural way to proceed (Parsons, 2000: 13):

ID. An object a is said to be *indeterminate*$_{\text{ID}}$ if there is something b such that it is indeterminate whether a is b (i.e., $\nabla(a = b)$).

For example, let k be a sharply defined mountain-shaped section of Earth's crust occupying the region where the most detailed maps of Tanzania locate Kilimanjaro. Is Kilimanjaro identical with k? Provided that it has been suitably selected, k is certainly as good a Kilimanjaro candidate as anything else. But no matter how much time we spend studying the maps, or interviewing the locals, or carrying out geological studies of the region, we will never be able to conclusively establish whether Kilimanjaro is k. In fact, it is not even clear how one could settle with outmost precision whether Kilimanjaro indeed is k, rather than some other sharply defined mountain-shaped item k' in that neighborhood. How so? Presumably because there is no fact of the matter whether Kilimanjaro is k rather than k' – in other words, because Kilimanjaro is indeterminate$_{\text{ID}}$ (see Figure 1).

Or consider an amoeba, Anne, splitting into two indistinguishable daughter cells, Betty and Claire. Assuming that Anne survives the mitotic process and

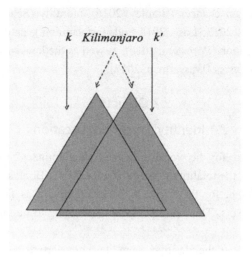

Figure 1 Indeterminacy$_{\text{ID}}$

that survival involves identity, which of the daughter cells is Anne? Certainly not both, on pain of inconsistency. On the other hand, identifying Anne with Betty rather than Claire, or the other way around, breaks the symmetry built into the example and reeks of arbitrariness. Here is a third option: it is indeterminate whether Anne is Betty, and it is indeterminate whether Anne is Claire. In compact form: it is indeterminate whether Anne is Betty or Claire. Thus, Anne is indeterminate$_{\text{ID}}$ and so are the daughters.

As it turns out, although ID provides what appears to be a seemingly plausible necessary condition for object indeterminacy, it cannot provide adequate sufficient conditions. We said that Kilimanjaro is indeterminate$_{\text{ID}}$ insofar as it is indeterminately identical with k. But since identity is symmetric, so is indeterminate identity. It follows that k is indeterminately identical with Kilimanjaro, and so that k is also indeterminate$_{\text{ID}}$. This has to be the wrong result, however, for the sharpness of k was built into our thought experiment. It appears therefore that ID overgenerates instances of object indeterminacy.

If ID causes trouble, perhaps some other condition in that vicinity will fare better. The reason the identity relation seemed like a good candidate for characterizing object indeterminacy is that it provides a way to individuate things. For example, the current president of the United Nations can be individuated by observing that he is Csaba Kőrösi. So any alternative characterization should arguably involve a relation that, like identity, suffices to individuate objects but that, unlike identity, is asymmetric. Such a role is satisfied by any asymmetric relation having the property of *extensionality*. One such relation is parthood on its classical construal.[1] Parthood is indeed asymmetric: a is a part of b only if b is not a part of a. Moreover, it is arguably *extensional* (Cotnoir & Varzi, 2021: 70). Call an object *atomic* if it has no parts. Parthood is extensional if the following is determinately the case:

EXT$_P$. Nonatomic objects having the same parts are identical
(i.e., $\forall x \forall y (\exists w Pwx \rightarrow \forall z ((Pzx \leftrightarrow Pzy) \rightarrow x = y)$, where Pxy stands for 'x is a part of y').

Insofar as an object is individuated by its parts, if any, we can formulate an alternative notion of object indeterminacy as follows (Burgess, 1990):

P. An object a is said to be *indeterminate$_P$* if there is something b such that it is indeterminate whether b is a part of a (i.e., $\nabla(Pba)$).

Since Kilimanjaro is nonatomic, and it is indeterminate whether it is identical with k, EXT$_P$ guarantees that it is also indeterminate whether Kilimanjaro and k have the same parts. Insofar as it is determinate which are the parts of k, there must be something b such that it is indeterminate whether it is a part of Kilimanjaro. Hence, Kilimanjaro is indeterminate$_P$. Furthermore, parthood being asymmetric, P does not make b indeterminate$_P$, and so is not inadequate in the way ID is.

One problem with P is that although it may provide sufficient conditions for something to be indeterminate, it does not seem to give us the right necessary conditions insofar as not every instance of object indeterminacy can be traced back to facts about parthood. A specific worry is that, even conceding that the indeterminacy of parthood tracks the indeterminacy of macroscopic objects, that does not carry over to the microscopic scale (Lewis, 2016: 72). Following Lowe (1994), consider an electron a that is absorbed by an atom M and becomes entangled with M's other electrons. After some time, M emits electron b. Because orthodox quantum mechanics tells us that particles lack determinate trajectories in space-time, there is no fact of the matter whether electrons a and b are one and the same electron. If so, a is indeterminate$_{ID}$, although not indeterminate$_P$.[2]

Is there any other asymmetric and extensional relation that could help us characterize object indeterminacy? Let us consider location, the relation

---

[1] By "parthood," I mean what is sometimes referred to as "proper parthood," thus a relation that is (at the very least) irreflexive, asymmetric, and transitive.

[2] French and Krause (2006) have developed a *quasi-set theory* wherein quantum particles lack (self-)identity altogether. If so, we would be facing a case of indefiniteness, rather than indeterminacy (cf. Darby, 2014). Alternatively, the lesson of quantum mechanics could be overridden by endowing particles with a primitive this-ness, thus making them determinate$_{ID}$.

holding between an object and each space-time region it exactly occupies. What I call location is what Parsons (2007) refers to as "exact location" – except that I am going to allow objects to be multi-located, so as to make room for the endurantist view that things persist by existing at multiple times.

Location is typically taken to be asymmetric: if something x is located at a region y, then y is not located at x (Simons, 2004: 345).[3] It is also often assumed, either implicitly or explicitly, that material objects are impenetrable in the sense that no two of them can exactly occupy the same space-time regions. Let us assume, then, that the following is determinately the case:

EXT_L. Objects having the same locations are identical
  (i.e., $\forall x \forall y (\forall z((Lxz \leftrightarrow Lyz) \rightarrow x = y)$, where Lxy stands for 'x is located at y').

This thesis captures the idea that material objects are individuated by their locations. Consider now the following location-based characterization of object indeterminacy:

L. An object a is said to be *indeterminate$_L$* if there is a space-time region r such that it is indeterminate whether a is located at r (i.e., $\nabla(Lar)$).

As it turns out, L can account for the indeterminacy of electrons once Lowe's example is suitably redescribed. Let r be the space-time region where electron a is located right before absorption, and s be the space-time region where electron b is located right after emission. According to orthodox quantum mechanics, there is no fact of the matter whether a is also located at s. So electron a is indeterminate$_L$ in that there is a region such that it is indeterminate whether a is located at it. Electron b is likewise indeterminate$_L$ in that it is indeterminate whether it is located at r. Moreover, if it is indeterminate whether a is b, as per Lowe's original formulation, EXT_L entails that it is also indeterminate whether a and b are colocated.

Similar conclusions can be drawn for the macroscopic case of Kilimanjaro. Since this is, unlike Lowe's, synchronic, we are allowed to assume that k has a unique location r, and by hypothesis that it has it determinately. If it is indeterminate whether Kilimanjaro is k, EXT_L guarantees that it is indeterminate whether Kilimanjaro and k are colocated and so whether Kilimanjaro is located at r. Hence, Kilimanjaro is indeterminate$_L$.

In conclusion, L seems to fare better than P when it comes to characterizing indeterminacy of material objects insofar as location in space-time is a property

---

[3] Location will be trivially symmetric if for a material object to be located at a region is for it to be identical with that region. This view, known as *supersubstantivalism*, is defended in Schaffer (2009). Also, see Casati and Varzi (1999: 119) for a nonasymmetric construal of location.

that is found at both macroscopic and microscopic scales in all physical theories, and is even regarded as fundamental in some of them, such as Bohmian mechanics. On the other hand, it is not clear that the parthood relation of classical mereology has any significance at the microscopic scale, in that it does not figure as a physical property in our fundamental physics (Ladyman & Ross, 2007: ch. 1).

A potential limitation of L is that it does not cover the case of objects (if any) that do not live in space-time, such as the abstract entities of mathematics. Consider the universe of sets as defined by Zermelo-Fraenkel first-order set theory with the axiom of choice (ZFU). German mathematician Georg Cantor (1878) conjectured that the cardinality of the real numbers ($2^{\aleph_0}$) is the smallest uncountable cardinal ($\aleph_1$), a thesis that went down in history as the *continuum hypothesis* (CH):[4]

$$2^{\aleph_0} = \aleph_1.$$

As was later demonstrated, however, CH is undecidable in that it can be neither disproved (Gödel, 1940) nor proved (Cohen, 1963) within ZFU.

How does that bit of history of mathematics bear on the question of object indeterminacy? Suppose that the way things are set-theoretically is uniquely specified by ZFU in such a way that, for every sentence 'p' in the language of first-order set theory, it is determinately the case that p if and only if 'p' is a theorem of ZFU. Due to CH's undecidability, it follows that it is neither determinately the case that $2^{\aleph_0} = \aleph_1$ nor determinately the case that $2^{\aleph_0} \neq \aleph_1$. Moreover, set membership ($\in$) is extensional, as per the following axiom of ZFU:

EXT$_{\text{SET}}$. Sets that have the same members are identical
(i.e., $\forall x \forall y (\forall z ((z \in x \leftrightarrow z \in y) \rightarrow x = y))$).

Therefore, if it is indeterminate whether $2^{\aleph_0} = \aleph_1$, then it is also indeterminate whether $2^{\aleph_0}$ and $\aleph_1$ are co-extensional. But sets are co-extensional if and only if they have the same subsets,[5] and the subsets of a set are none other than its parts (Lewis, 1991). Consequently, it is indeterminate whether $2^{\aleph_0}$ and $\aleph_1$ have the same parts, which means that at least one of them is indeterminate$_P$. So the undecidability of CH relative to ZFU entails the existence of mereologically

---

[4] Technically, CH states that there is no mapping from the reals onto $\aleph_2$. Within ZFU, the official statement is equivalent with the identity statement '$2^{\aleph_0} = \aleph_1$'.

[5] If sets a, b are co-extensional, by EXT$_{\text{SET}}$ they are identical and so have the same subsets. Conversely, if they are not co-extensional, then there is something c which is a member of a and not b (or the other way around), and so the singleton $\{c\}$ is a subset of a and not b (or the other way around).

indeterminate sets, provided that the way things are is specified by ZFU.[6] Yet there is no way to capture the indeterminacy of (pure) sets in terms of L insofar as they are not located in space-time.[7]

To be sure, set-theoretic indeterminacy is not forced upon us by the undecidability of CH, since the assumption that ZFU (or some other axiomatization) determines the way things are set-theoretically could reasonably be rejected. Platonists such as Gödel have taken the independence result to mean that ZFU is unable to completely describe the One True set-theoretic universe. On this view, there is a perfectly determinate, mind-independent structure that can be captured more or less adequately depending on one's choice of axioms.

An even bolder form of Platonism is committed to a set-theoretic multiverse wherein the different universes satisfy alternative set-theoretic theses (Hamkins, 2012). On this view, there is a region of the multiverse that makes both ZFU and CH true, and one that makes ZFU true and CH false. Indeterminacy is nowhere to be found – not at the fundamental level of the multiverse, at least. In conclusion, whether set-theoretic undecidability leads to object indeterminacy, and to metaphysical indeterminacy at large, depends on broader questions in the philosophy of mathematics.

2.2 All Roads Lead to Identity

So far, we have been unable to find a characterization of object indeterminacy that applies to all putative cases – macroscopic, microscopic, as well as abstract objects. One may be tempted to look for some other asymmetric and extensional relation that could play the relevant role, or else produce some disjunctive characterization in terms of the relations considered so far.[8]

Be that as it may, any such proposal is bound to face a major challenge. In order to see that, let us start by observing that something is indeterminate$_P$ only if it is indeterminate$_{ID}$. Without loss of generality, we may consider the case of the indeterminate$_P$ object Kilimanjaro. Suppose that Kilimanjaro is determinately composed of $k_1, \ldots, k_n$, and indeterminately composed of k_{n+1}. Also, suppose that the mountain-like object k, which is not indeterminate$_P$, is determinately composed of $k_1, \ldots, k_n, k_{n+1}$. In other words, Kilimanjaro and k differ only in that the latter does whereas the former does not determinately has k_{n+1} as

---

[6] Barnes and Williams (2011: 70) also make a case for metaphysical indeterminacy arising from CH.

[7] Whether L could be generalized to an object's location in some abstract space is an open question.

[8] A weaker notion of object indeterminacy, which need not involve any extensional relation, is articulated in Smith and Rosen (2004). Such cases are subsumed by the class of theories discussed in Section 3.

a part. Now, if k_{n+1} is not a part of Kilimanjaro, then Kilimanjaro and k are distinct, and if k_{n+1} is a part of Kilimanjaro, then Kilimanjaro and k have the same parts and so are, by EXT$_P$, identical. Thus, Kilimanjaro and k are identical if and only if k_{n+1} is a part of Kilimanjaro. Since it is indeterminate whether k_{n+1} is a part of Kilimanjaro, it is also indeterminate whether Kilimanjaro and k are identical. It must be concluded that Kilimanjaro is indeterminate$_{ID}$ (cf. Weatherson, 2003; Barnes & Williams, 2009).[9]

Insofar as this line of reasoning applies not just to Kilimanjaro but to all sorts of scenarios involving indeterminate$_P$ objects, the moral to be drawn is that indeterminacy of parthood entails indeterminate identity. Moreover, because the key assumption is the extensionality of parthood, the reasoning carries over, *mutatis mutandis*, to any other notion of object indeterminacy that is characterized in terms of some extensional relation.

2.3 Against Indeterminate Identity

As we just saw, each one of the notions of object indeterminacy considered so far has turned out to involve indeterminate identity, whether explicitly or implicitly. In a much-discussed one-page article, Evans (1978) argued that indeterminate identity is incoherent. The argument is as follows.

1. It is indeterminate whether a is b (i.e., $\nabla(a = b)$)   [Premise](1).
2. b is such that it is indeterminate whether a is it
   (i.e., $\langle \lambda x. \nabla(a = x) \rangle b$)   [1](1).
3. It is not indeterminate whether a is a (i.e., $\neg \nabla(a = a)$).
4. a is not such that it is indeterminate whether a is it
   (i.e., $\neg \langle \lambda x. \nabla(a = x) \rangle a$)   [3].
5. a is not b (i.e., $\neg(a = b)$)   [2,4](1).

The argument purports to show that the hypothesis that it is indeterminate whether a is b entails that a is not b, which is supposed to undermine the hypothesis.

Line 1 is the assumption to be disproved. The inference from 1 to 2 is due to the *β-expansion* rule of lambda calculus, which captures the inference from *de dicto* to *de re* predication:

$$\phi[t] \vdash \langle \lambda x. \phi[x] \rangle t.$$

Informally, the rule says that if t is so-and-so, then t has the property of being so-and-so (or: t is such that it is so-and-so).

---

[9] The argument hinges on classical logic, which is invalid on some accounts of metaphysical indeterminacy, most notably many-valued logics (Section 3.2.1). The same conclusion can nevertheless be reached in a many-valued setting from the premise that objects are identical iff they have the same parts.

Line 3 follows from $\mathbf{D}(a = a)$, which is obtained from the logical truth $a = a$ via the metarule of *determination* (the analog of *necessitation*),

if $\vdash \phi$ then $\vdash \mathbf{D}\phi$

which is guaranteed to hold if '$\mathbf{D}$' defines a normal modal logic.

The inference from 3 to 4 is obtained by contraposition via the *β-reduction* rule of lambda calculus (the converse of *β*-expansion), which captures the inference from *de re* to *de dicto* predication:

$$\langle \lambda x.\phi[x] \rangle t \vdash \phi[t].$$

Informally, the rule of *β*-reduction says that if *t* has the property of being so-and-so (or: *t* is such that it is so-and-so), then *t* is so-and-so.

Finally, line 5 is obtained from 2 and 4 by contraposition via *Leibniz's Law*, the thesis that identical things have the same properties:

for every property *P*, from $a = b$ and *Pa* infer *Pb*

(i.e., $a = b, Pa \vdash Pb$).

The first thing to be noted is that the proof falls short of producing the inconsistency that a proper *reductio* demands. One might be tempted to round off the proof by appealing to the rule of $\mathbf{D}$-*introduction*

$$\phi \vdash \mathbf{D}\phi$$

which holds on some theories of (in)determinacy, namely those wherein '$\mathbf{D}$' maps true statements to true statements, and untrue statements to false statements (Parsons, 2000). By applying $\mathbf{D}$-introduction to line 5, we get $\mathbf{D}\neg(a = b)$, thus contradicting line 1. However, logics validating $\mathbf{D}$-introduction cannot bivalent, or else they would rule out indeterminacy, and when bivalence fails, so does contraposition, which the proof relies on (Section 2.4.1). So this strategy is out of the question.

The strategy that Evans recommends in order to complete the proof is to assume that '$\mathbf{D}$' defines a modal system S5, which validates the following schemas:

$$\mathbf{D}\phi \leftrightarrow \mathbf{DD}\phi$$

$$\neg\mathbf{D}\phi \leftrightarrow \mathbf{D}\neg\mathbf{D}\phi.$$

The gist of these equivalences is that facts about determinacy or lack thereof are determinate. We are then allowed to infer $\mathbf{D}\phi$ from each premise ϕ of Evans's argument. Moreover, in virtue of being a modal operator, '$\mathbf{D}$' is expected to validate the following metarule (Koslow, A. 1992):

if $\phi, \chi, \ldots \vdash \psi$ then $\mathbf{D}\phi, \mathbf{D}\chi, \ldots \vdash \mathbf{D}\psi,$

capturing the sensible thesis that determinate truth is closed under entailment. We can therefore derive $\mathbf{D}\neg(a = b)$, which explicitly contradicts $\nabla a = b$.

The problem with Evans's strategy is that it is far from uncontroversial that S5 is the logic of determinacy. Two kinds of reasons have been adduced against that thesis. First, S5 is incompatible with the phenomenon of *higher-order indeterminacy* (Williamson, 1999). First-order indeterminacy as to whether ϕ is the existence of a gap between what is determinately ϕ and what is determinately non-ϕ; second-order indeterminacy as to whether ϕ is the existence of a gap between what is determinately determinately ϕ and what is determinately indeterminately ϕ, and between what is determinately indeterminately ϕ and what is determinately determinately non-ϕ, and so forth.

Higher-order indeterminacy arises with respect to sorites series, and vagueness at large. Because it seems absurd to think that there is a precise number of hairs separating the determinately bald from the determinately nonbald, we feel compelled to postulate cases of borderline baldness. Likewise, because it seems absurd to think that there is a precise number of hairs separating the determinately determinately bald from the determinately indeterminately bald, or the determinately indeterminately bald from the determinately determinately nonbald, we are compelled to postulate borderline borderline baldness, and so forth.

Insofar as vagueness involves higher-order indeterminacy, the logic of 'D' cannot be as strong as S5. Does this fact undermine Evans's strategy to complete the *reductio*? Arguably not, since vagueness cannot arise in the language of Evans's *reductio*, which includes only individual constants and logical vocabulary. Indeed, a sorites series for the predicate $\langle \lambda x.\text{Kilimanjaro} = x \rangle$ would have to run from a determinate$_{\text{ID}}$ object a satisfying $\langle \lambda x.\mathbf{D}\neg(\text{Kilimanjaro} = x) \rangle$ to a determinate$_{\text{ID}}$ object b satisfying $\langle \lambda x.\mathbf{D}(\text{Kilimanjaro} = x) \rangle$. But the existence of such a b is provably incompatible with Kilimanjaro's being indeterminate$_{\text{ID}}$.[10] So Evans can rely on S5 for the purpose of his argument.

A wholly different kind of considerations against S5 have been put forward by Akiba (2014a), who has defended a theory of metaphysical indeterminacy wherein the B schema $\phi \rightarrow \mathbf{D}\neg\mathbf{D}\neg\phi$ is invalid. Since that schema is an axiom of S5, Akiba concludes that the *reductio* cannot be carried out. I will return to this response to Evans in Section 2.4.5, and to Akiba's theory of metaphysical indeterminacy at large in Section 3.3.2.

---

[10] Proof. Suppose that (i) $\mathbf{D}\neg(\text{Kilimanjaro} = a)$ and (ii) $\mathbf{D}(\text{Kilimanjaro} = b)$. Due to the absence of sharp cutoffs in the series, there must be something c such that $\nabla(\text{Kilimanjaro} = c)$, and so (iii) $\neg\mathbf{D}\neg(\text{Kilimanjaro} = c)$. Because b and c are determinate$_{\text{ID}}$, as well as distinct elements of the series, (iv) $\mathbf{D}\neg(b = c)$. By ii and iii, $\neg\mathbf{D}\neg(b = c)$. Contradiction.

2.4 Resisting Evans

2.4.1 Contraposition

We have seen Evans's argument against indeterminate$_\text{ID}$ objects, as well as a way to extend it to a proper *reductio*. Whether the argument is conclusive is the subject of a sophisticated and relatively sizeable literature. I am now going to present a number of routes that the friend of indeterminate objects can take.

The first and perhaps most straightforward line of resistance is based on the observation that the argument relies on the metarule of *contraposition*,

$$\text{if } \phi, \chi, \dots \vdash \psi \text{ then } \phi, \neg\psi, \dots \vdash \neg\chi,$$

which, although classically valid, ceases to be uncontroversial when (in)determinacy is involved (Frege, 1903: 65; Williamson, 1994: 151; Keefe, 2000: 179). For example, the inference from 'Bob is bald' to 'it is determinate that Bob is bald', an instance of **D**-introduction, is valid on many a theory of metaphysical indeterminacy – although there are voices of dissent (Akiba, 2014a, 2022; Barnes & Williams, 2011). On the other hand, inferring 'Bob is not bald' from 'it is not determinate that Bob is bald' is a non sequitur.

Unlike contraposition, the following metarule of *weak contraposition* is universally accepted:

$$\text{if } \phi, \chi, \dots \vdash \psi \text{ then } \phi, \neg\psi, \dots \vdash \neg\mathbf{D}\chi.$$

Weak contraposition, however, is too weak to validate Evans's argument. In particular, the weak contrapositive of Leibniz's Law licenses the following conclusion on line 5:

it is not determinate that a is not b (i.e., $\neg\mathbf{D}(a = b)$),

which is clearly compatible with the argument's premises.

Williamson (2003a: 708) and Williams (2008a: 137) have objected that the contrapositive of Leibniz's Law feels as compelling as the uncontraposed formulation. If that is the case, we are entitled to add it as an extra primitive rule, even when contraposition at large is invalid, thus restoring the argument's validity.

There are two reasons to be skeptical of such a move. First, the contrapositive of Leibniz's Law is not nearly as compelling as the standard rule when (in)determinacy is involved, especially in the class of cases we have been discussing. For the following inference is unassailable:

Kilimanjaro is k

It is determinate that j is a part of k

Therefore, it is determinate that j is a part of Kilimanjaro.

On the other hand, its contrapositive,

> It is not determinate that j is a part of Kilimanjaro
> It is determinate that j is a part of k
> Therefore, Kilimanjaro is not k

is precisely the kind of argument that one might find uncompelling. For if Kilimanjaro and k only differ as to which parts they determinately have, the friend of indeterminate objects will take that to be evidence that they are not determinately identical, rather than nonidentical. Appealing to intuitions about the logic of identity is hardly going to move the needle of the discussion.

The second reason to be skeptical is that Evans's proof applies contraposition not only to Leibniz's Law but also to β-reduction, namely in the step from line 3 to line 4. So leveraging our intuitions about identity is not going to suffice anyway. Moreover, intuitions about β-reduction are arguably not nearly as clear-cut as intuitions about identity. Therefore, contraposed β-reduction is going to be as controversial as contraposed Leibniz's Law, if not more.

2.4.2 Reference

The second line of resistance to Evans's argument questions his appeal to β-expansion and β-reduction, which, although classically valid, may fail when intensional notions such as necessity, knowledge, and determinacy are involved (Lewis, 1988). In order to see that, it will be helpful to reason by analogy with metaphysical modality. Insofar as things in the solar system could have turned out otherwise, the following *de dicto* statement is true:

> It is contingent whether the number of planets is 8.

Assuming that 'the number of planets' is a referential term, an application of β-expansion yields the *de re* statement

> The number of planets is such that it is contingent whether it is 8.

However, the latter is false, for it and the true statement 'the number of planets is 8' jointly entail, by Leibniz's Law, the false statement '8 is such that it is contingent whether it is 8'.

The familiar story is that *de dicto* to *de re* inferences such as this are warranted as long as the term being outscoped is *rigid* – that is, it has constant interpretation across worlds. Rigidity can be characterized modally by means of the following condition ('**N**' being the necessity operator):

> 't' is rigid iff something is necessarily t (i.e., $\exists x \mathbf{N}(x = t)$).[11]

---

[11] In order to avoid irrelevant complications, I will be assuming that 't' refers necessarily.

Because the number of planets may vary, 'the number of planets' is nonrigid, which explains why the foregoing application of β-expansion is not truth-preserving. Similar considerations carry over to β-reduction.

Let us now assume that 'it is determinate that' (**D**) is analogous to 'it is necessary that' (**N**), and 'it is indeterminate whether' (∇) is analogous to 'it is contingent whether'. We can then introduce the notion of *referential determinacy* by analogy with rigidity:

'*t*' is referentially determinate iff something is determinately *t* (i.e., $\exists x \mathbf{D}(x = t)$).

The aforementioned restrictions on β-expansion and β-reduction apply *mutatis mutandis* to inferences involving (in)determinacy talk. For example, the step from 'it is indeterminate whether *k* is Kilimanjaro' to 'Kilimanjaro is such that it is indeterminate whether *k* is it' is warranted as long as the term being outscoped, 'Kilimanjaro', is referentially determinate.

There are two ways for a term to be referentially indeterminate. First, we could be dealing with run-of-the-mill semantic indeterminacy, which arises whenever the linguistic conventions underlying our use of a term like 'Kilimanjaro' are not sufficiently stringent to narrow down a single candidate referent, in much the same way as the conventions underlying our use of 'tall' fail to pick out a single candidate property (Noonan, 1982). If that is indeed the case, the sentence 'Kilimanjaro is *k*' will express an instance of *de dicto* semantic indeterminacy. The indeterminacy arises because the two terms are not determinately co-referring; it is semantic because it is grounded in facts about language; and it is *de dicto* because 'Kilimanjaro' is referentially indeterminate.

Williams (2008a: 151–152) has argued that referential indeterminacy can also arise as the result of worldly, rather than semantic, indeterminacy. Applied to our running example, the argument goes as follows. Suppose that Kilimanjaro is indeterminate$_L$ in that there is no fact of the matter whether it shares its location with the precise mountain-like object *k*, rather than some other precise mountain-like object *k'*. The name 'Kilimanjaro' will then be referentially indeterminate between *k* and *k'*. According to this reading, 'Kilimanjaro is *k*' expresses an instance of *de dicto* metaphysical indeterminacy. The indeterminacy arises because 'Kilimanjaro' and '*k*' are not determinately co-referring; it is metaphysical because it is grounded in facts about Kilimanjaro's location; and it is *de dicto* because 'Kilimanjaro' is referentially indeterminate.

If Williams is right, statements of indeterminacy with a metaphysical source need not be *de re*. This diagnosis offers a way out of Evans's proof by resisting the β-expansion step. If indeterminacy is analogous to contingency, 'Kilimanjaro is such that it is indeterminate whether k is it' can be inferred from 'It is indeterminate whether Kilimanjaro is k' provided that 'something is determinately identical with Kilimanjaro' is true, which is not the case if 'Kilimanjaro' is referentially indeterminate. Conclusion: although *de re* identity statements cannot be indeterminate, *de dicto* identity statements can be indeterminate in virtue of the way the world is.

As it turns out, Williams's line of reasoning is dialectically ineffective. One of his key motivations for introducing *de dicto* indeterminate identities with a metaphysical source is that they provide a way to respond to Evans without giving up contraposition, or any other classical form of inference. Now, suppose for the sake of argument that the strategy is vindicated and that Evans's proof can be resisted because 'Kilimanjaro' is referentially indeterminate. As a consequence, we will have to deny the truth of $\exists x \mathbf{D}(x = \text{Kilimanjaro})$. This, however, follows by the classical rule of existential generalization

$$\phi[t] \vdash \exists x \phi[x]$$

from $\mathbf{D}(\text{Kilimanjaro} = \text{Kilimanjaro})$, which is a logical truth provided that (i) Kilimanjaro = Kilimanjaro is a logical truth, and that (ii) '$\mathbf{D}$' defines a normal modal logic. Because Williams (2008a: 136) is wedded to classical logic, he must accept both i and classical existential generalization. Moreover, if determinacy is analogous to metaphysical necessity, ii is also guaranteed. In fact, in Barnes and Williams (2011: 135), a case is made for the stronger thesis that the logic of '$\mathbf{D}$' defines a modal system S5. It must be concluded that the way Williams attempts to resist Evans is incompatible with his own logical desiderata.

Williams might reply by observing that *de dicto* indeterminacy is semantic in character, even when grounded in worldly rather than linguistic matters. So a language $\mathcal{L}$ tasked with expressing instances of worldly indeterminacy need not be able to state *de dicto* indeterminate statements. Once referentially indeterminate terms are expunged from $\mathcal{L}$, statements involving such terms can no longer be stated, thus restoring classical logic.

The reply misses the mark. If $\mathcal{L}$ is a language for talking about indeterminate subject matters, and location is one of them, then 'Kilimanjaro is colocated with k' must be statable in $\mathcal{L}$ – which of course is impossible if 'Kilimanjaro' is not a term of $\mathcal{L}$. Thus, any language tasked with describing indeterminate subject matters will either fail to validate classical logic or be expressively incomplete.

2.4.3 Impredicativity

Parsons (2000, 50–54) also believes that Evans goes wrong in taking
β-expansion for granted, although he denies any analogy between indeterminacy and contingency. Rather, he thinks that the β-expansion step is invalid
because the predicate $\langle \lambda x.\nabla(a = x)\rangle$ fails to express a property, and so it cannot
be plugged into Leibniz's Law as the proof requires.

This strategy involves two steps. The first is the diagnosis of the problem,
which Parsons identifies with the impredicativity of $\langle \lambda x.\nabla(a = x)\rangle$. An expression is said to be *impredicative* if it is defined by quantifying over a domain of
objects that includes that expression's putative semantic value. During the
debate on the logical foundations of mathematics in the early twentieth century,
impredicativity came under fire because it was involved in Russell's paradox of
naïve set theory, as well as other challenges to the logicist project. Indeed, the
unrestricted axiom of comprehension guarantees the existence of the set R of all
sets that are not self-membered:

$$\forall x(x \in R \leftrightarrow \neg(x \in x)).$$

But R's existence is contradictory, since it entails the truth-functional
falsehood

$$R \in R \leftrightarrow \neg(R \in R).$$

Russell among others was convinced that impredicativity was the culprit and
addressed the problem by purging it from the theory of sets.

According to Parsons, a similar moral applies to Evans's proof. Insofar
as identity is second-order definable as the relation that a bears to b just in
case a and b have the exact same properties, the predicate $\langle \lambda x.\nabla(a = x)\rangle$
reduces to $\langle \lambda x.\nabla \forall P(Pa \leftrightarrow Px)\rangle$. If the latter predicate expresses a property,
this must be in the range of the universal quantifier occurring in the
predicate itself. Parsons concludes that, by rejecting impredicative definitions, Evans's proof can be resisted and the coherence of indeterminate
identity upheld.

Parsons then proceeds to identify a suitable condition that should rule out the
troublemaking predicates. Say that a formula $\phi[x]$ *determinately distinguishes*
objects a and b just in case it is determinately satisfied by a, and determinately
not satisfied by b (i.e., $\mathbf{D}\phi[a]$ and $\mathbf{D}\neg\phi[b]$), or vice versa. Parsons assumes the
following postulate:

DD. $\langle \lambda x.\phi[x]\rangle$ expresses a property only if $\phi[x]$ does not determinately distin-
    guish objects that are indeterminately identical.

DD guarantees that predicates of the form $\langle \lambda x.\nabla(a = x)\rangle$ fail to pick out any properties. In order to see that, let $\phi[x]$ be $\nabla(k = x)$, and suppose that

$$\nabla(k = \text{Kilimanjaro}).$$

It follows by **D**-introduction (which Parson's logic validates) that

$$\mathbf{D}\nabla(k = \text{Kilimanjaro}).$$

On the other hand, $\mathbf{D}(k = k)$ entails $\neg\nabla(k = k)$ and so, by another application of **D**-introduction,

$$\mathbf{D}\neg\nabla(k = k).$$

So $\phi[x]$ determinately distinguishes Kilimanjaro and k, against DD.

The cogency of Parsons's strategy rests on his diagnosis of the alleged flaw in Evans's proof, namely its reliance on impredicative definitions. However, there are reasons to be skeptical of such a diagnosis. First of all, there are properties that are impredicative yet do not cause any trouble. For example, the property of being Kilimanjaro (i.e., $\langle \lambda x.\text{Kilimanjaro} = x\rangle$) is defined by means of identity and so is just as impredicative as the property of being indeterminately identical with Kilimanjaro (i.e., $\langle \lambda x.\nabla(\text{Kilimanjaro} = x)\rangle$). But whereas the latter is ruled out by DD, the former isn't.

Conversely, call a predicate *haecceitistic* if it is both semantically irreducible and true of just one particular object – for example, the predicate 'Socratize' (cf. Quine, 1948). DD rules out the property of being such that it indeterminately Kilimanjarizes (i.e., $\langle \lambda x.\nabla \text{Kilimanjarize}(x)\rangle$), which is co-intensional with the property of being indeterminately identical with Kilimanjaro, and so will determinately distinguish Kilimanjaro and k. However, this property is not impredicative, since it is defined by means of the haecceitistic predicate 'Kilimanjarize', which is semantically irreducible and so involves no covert quantification over properties.

The moral is that impredicativity neither entails nor is entailed by the class of predicates that DD singles out as semantically vacuous, which suggests that impredicativity is a red herring.

2.4.4 Counterparts

The fourth line of resistance I wish to consider hinges on the analogy between determinacy and necessity, together with the counterpart-theoretic interpretation of modal discourse developed in Lewis (1968).

Counterpart theory differs from standard Kripke semantics in the way it handles *de re* predication. The standard approach, which is formulated against a background ontology of trans-world individuals, satisfies the following biconditionals:

'It is possible that *a* is *P*' is true iff, for some world *w*, '*a* is *P*' is true at *w*.
'It is necessary that *a* is *P*' is true iff, for every world *w*, '*a* is *P*' is true at *w*.

The Lewisian approach, on the other hand, construes modal predication by means of counterpart relations. A counterpart relation is a relation of comparative similarity: the *w*-counterparts of something *a* are the individuals of *w* that most resemble *a* both intrinsically and extrinsically. Lewis's paraphrase from modal language to the language of counterpart theory satisfies the following biconditionals:

'It is possible that *a* is *P*' is true iff, for some world *w* and *w*-counterpart *a** of *a*, '*a** is *P*' is true at *w*.
'It is necessary that *a* is *P*' is true iff, for every world *w* and *w*-counterpart *a** of *a*, '*a** is *P*' is true at *w*.

Accordingly, for Socrates to possibly fail to be a philosopher is tantamount to there being a world in which some counterpart of Socrates is not a philosopher.

One of the advertised virtues of counterpart theory is that it addresses some puzzles of material constitution by appealing to the inconstancy of *de re* predication (Lewis, 1986: 248). By way of illustration, imagine a statue of clay representing the biblical giant Goliath (Gibbard, 1975). Let 'Goliath' be the name of the statue and 'Lumpl' be the name of the lump of clay constituting it. Insofar as Lumpl and Goliath occupy the exact same regions, they are identical (by EXT_L). On the other hand, they arguably instantiate different modal properties: Lumpl can and Goliath cannot survive being flattened. By Leibniz's Law, we are compelled to conclude that Lumpl and Goliath are nonidentical. Contradiction.

The Lewisian solution appeals to the fact that the truth conditions of a given *de re* modal statement involve a counterpart relation, and that different contexts of utterance may prompt different counterpart relations. In particular, by uttering

Goliath could survive being flattened

we ascribe a modal property to something being referred to by a name for things falling under the statue sortal. In other words, we are predicating something of Goliath *qua* statue. The statement's truth conditions – says Lewis – should then be specified in terms of a counterpart relation R_1 that selects objects resembling Goliath *qua* statue. A flattened piece of clay in no way resembles a statue and therefore cannot be a counterpart of Goliath. So it is not the case that Goliath could survive being flattened.

On the other hand, an utterance of

Lumpl could survive being flattened

ascribes a modal property to something being referred to by a name for things falling under the clay sortal. In other words, we are predicating something of Lumpl *qua* lump of clay. The statement's truth conditions will then have to be specified in terms of a counterpart relation R_2 that selects objects resembling Lumpl *qua* lump of clay. A flattened piece of clay can resemble Lumpl closely enough to be its counterpart. Therefore, Lumpl could survive being flattened.

The moral of Lewis's strategy is that the interpretation of the predicate 'could survive being flattened' is contextual, in that it depends on a choice of counterpart relation. Consequently, we cannot apply Leibniz's Law and conclude that Lumpl is not Goliath, since 'could survive being flattened' fails to pick out a property that Lumpl does and Goliath does not have (or vice versa).

Barnes (2009) has defended a similar strategy in order to resist Evans's proof. First, suppose that '**D**' ranges over ways of making reality precise, aka ontic precisifications, which Barnes identifies with possible worlds. (On this construal of (in)determinacy, see Section 3.3.) Second, assume a counterpart-theoretic construal of (in)determinacy statements, to the effect that the following biconditional will hold:

'It is determinate that a is P' is true iff, for every ontic precisification w and w-counterpart a^* of a, 'a^* is P' is true at w.

Now we suppose that

Kilimanjaro is determinately identical with k

is false, as the friend of indeterminate objects wants us to believe, whereas

k is determinately identical with k

is true. We cannot – says Barnes – apply Leibniz's Law and conclude that Kilimanjaro is not k, since the predicate 'is determinately identical with k' expresses different properties depending on the context of utterance: in the first utterance, it is interpreted relative to a counterpart relation prompted by the term 'Kilimanjaro', whereas in the second, it is interpreted relative to a counterpart relation prompted by the term 'k'. Thus, on a counterpart-theoretic construal of *de re* (in)determinacy, Evans's argument is invalid.

However, there are two important disanalogies between Lewis's argument for the inconstancy of modal properties and Barnes's argument for indeterminate identities. First, in the Lewisian scenario, the different counterpart relations are invoked by the use of names associated with different sortals: the

statue sortal for 'Goliath' versus the clay sortal for 'Lumpl'. That feature of
Lewis's argument is missing in Evans-style scenarios. Indeed, 'Kilimanjaro'
is a name for a mountain, and 'k' is a name that was introduced to pick out
a mountain-like object. Insofar as there is no qualitative difference between
mountains and mountain-like objects, it is safe to assume that mountains just
are mountain-like objects, and so the names 'Kilimanjaro' and 'k' are associated with the same sortals. Therefore, Barnes cannot replicate Lewis's strategy
and appeal to sortal differences in order to introduce different counterpart
relations depending on whether the subject of predication is 'Kilimanjaro' as
opposed to 'k'.

The second disanalogy is of a more technical nature. Whereas Barnes
claims to be giving a counterpart-theoretic interpretation of indeterminacy
statements, Lewis's own theory does not include a clause to paraphrase
sentences involving predicate abstracts, which play a crucial role in Evans's
argument – nor does Barnes provide one of her own. The Lewisian diagnosis
of puzzles of material composition is indeed formulated in a modal language
without predicate abstraction. Therefore, the claim that the complex predicate
'is determinately identical with k' is context-dependent is unjustified, since we
don't know how to interpret statements of the form $\langle \lambda x.\phi \rangle a$ counterpart-
theoretically.

Can the Lewisian paraphrase scheme be suitably extended so as to cover such
statements? It is unclear. If 'p' is a statement in some intensional target
language, let 'p^C' be its counterpart-theoretic paraphrase. For example:

(Determinately, Hesperus is not Phosphorus)^C = For every ontic precisification
    w, every w-counterpart H* of Hesperus, and every w-counterpart P* of
    Phosphorus, H* is not P*.

Here is a way of extending the Lewisian paraphrase to sentences involving
predicate abstracts:

$$(\langle \lambda x.\phi \rangle a)^C = \langle \lambda x.\phi^C a \rangle.$$

The obvious problem with this clause is that, by making the interpretation of the
predicate independent of the argument 'a', it is useless for the purpose of
Barnes's strategy.

An alternative clause is the following:

$$(\langle \lambda x.\phi \rangle a)^C = (\phi[x/a])^C.$$

By equating *de re* and *de dicto* predication, this solution makes β-expansion
redundant. One can then simplify Evans's argument by eliminating all applications of β-expansion and β-reduction:

1. It is indeterminate whether a is b (i.e., $\nabla(a = b)$). [Premise](1)
2. It is not indeterminate whether a is a (i.e., $\neg\nabla(a = a)$).
3. a is not b (i.e., $\neg(a = b)$). [1,2](1)

Since the simplified argument only involves one step, the only way to avoid the conclusion is by rejecting either Leibniz's Law or contraposition. Because the argument is paraphrased into counterpart theory, which is stated in a classical and bivalent logic, contraposition holds. Therefore, the advocate of indeterminate identities will have to regard Leibniz's Law as invalid. But this would be a desperate move insofar as Leibniz's Law is widely regarded as a defining condition for the identity relation, as Barnes (2009, 90n22) also seems to acknowledge. The second paraphrase strategy is not viable either.

What the friend of indeterminate identities actually needs is a clause to the effect that the predicate's semantic value is a function of the term(s) to which it is applied, namely:

$$(\langle \lambda x.\phi\rangle a)^C = \langle \lambda x.\phi^{C,a}\rangle a.$$

This last clause requires a substantive revision of the Lewisian paraphrase strategy, along lines which are yet unexplored. Whether such a route is viable remains an open problem.

2.4.5 Indeterminate Distinctness

It was observed in Section 2.3 that Evans's proof falls short of reaching a contradiction and needs therefore to be completed. Akiba (2014a) defends a theory of indeterminacy wherein such a completion does not exist. The reply consists of three steps: extending the overall argument so as to reach a contradiction; showing that the extension involves an extra premise; articulating and defending a theory of metaphysical indeterminacy that does not uphold that premise.

As to the first step, Akiba thinks that Evans's proof can be extended to a *reductio* in the following way (I am omitting here the natural language paraphrase):

1. $\nabla(a = b)$ [Premise](1)
   . . .   . . .
5. $\neg(a = b)$ [2,4](1)
6. $\neg(a = b) \rightarrow \mathbf{D}\neg(a = b)$ [Premise](6)
7. $\mathbf{D}\neg(a = b)$ [5,6](1,6)
8. $\neg\mathbf{D}\neg(a = b)$ [1](1)
9. $\neg\nabla(a = b)$ [1,7,8](6)

The extra premise is the *determinacy of distinctness* (line 6), which can be derived from the *determinacy of identity*, $a = b \rightarrow \mathbf{D}(a = b)$, plus some assumptions about the logic of determinacy. In order to see that, let us start by observing that the determinacy of identity has the following proof:

1. $a = b$ [Premise](1)
2. $\mathbf{D}(a = a)$
3. $\langle \lambda x.\mathbf{D}(a = x) \rangle a$ [2]
4. $\langle \lambda x.\mathbf{D}(a = x) \rangle b$ [1,3](1)
5. $\mathbf{D}(a = b)$ [4](1)
6. $a = b \rightarrow \mathbf{D}(a = b)$ [1,5]

Suppose now that $\mathbf{D}$ defines a modal system KB – that is, it validates a normal modal logic, as well as the B schema $\phi \rightarrow \mathbf{D}\neg\mathbf{D}\neg\phi$. One can then derive the determinacy of distinctness like so:

1. $\neg\mathbf{D}\neg\neg a = b \rightarrow \neg a = b$
2. $\mathbf{D}(\neg\mathbf{D}\neg\neg a = b \rightarrow \neg a = b)$ [1]
3. $\mathbf{D}\neg\mathbf{D}\neg\neg a = b \rightarrow \mathbf{D}\neg a = b$ [2]
4. $\neg a = b \rightarrow \mathbf{D}\neg\mathbf{D}\neg\neg a = b$
5. $\neg a = b \rightarrow \mathbf{D}\neg a = b$ [3,4]

Line 1 is a classical consequence of the determinacy of identity, and so a logical truth. Lines 2 and 3 are obtained via normality. Line 4 is an instance of the B schema. Line 5 is straightforward.

   Since normality is a fairly minimal assumption, the proof of the determinacy of distinctness is going to stand or fall on the B schema. Akiba articulates and defends a precisificational theory of metaphysical indeterminacy that does not uphold $\phi \rightarrow \mathbf{D}\neg\mathbf{D}\neg\phi$, thus blocking the *reductio* of indeterminate identities. Note that the same reply applies to Evans's preferred way of completing the proof, which appeals to the logic S5 and therefore hinges on the validity of the B schema.

   This is an interesting reply in that it questions not the five-line deduction that Evans provided, but the existence of a suitable completion. In order to assess this strategy, we need to delve into Akiba's theory of metaphysical indetermin-acy, which is postponed until Section 3.3.

2.5 Indeterminate Objects Sans Indeterminate Identity

Let us take stock. Evans's argument targets all characterizations of object indeterminacy that appeal to either indeterminate identity or the indeterminacy of properties (parthood, location, etc.) which, by satisfying an extensionality condition, give rise to indeterminate identity. The argument is as succinct as it is powerful, yet it is not irresistible. Indeed, we saw that there are quite a few strategies that the advocate of indeterminate identities may pursue – the simplest of them being to give up contraposition for languages that feature an (in) determinacy operator.

The advocate of indeterminate objects could nevertheless accept Evans's point by decoupling object indeterminacy from the truth of statements of the form $\nabla(a = b)$. One straightforward way of doing so is to take something as indeterminate just in case it is, say, mereologically indeterminate, as per P, while denying the extensionality of parthood. Indeed, although the parthood relation of classical mereology satisfies EXT_P, there is a sizeable literature challenging the received view. A typical example is that of two words, like 'part' and 'trap', which are composed of the same letter types (Hempel, 1953: 110). Although classical mereologists think that such alleged counterexamples to extensionality can be explained away, the view that parthood is not extensional is very much alive.

It is also possible to accept Evans's lesson and provide a characterization of object indeterminacy that neither entails indeterminate identities nor requires rejecting any of the standard extensionality conditions on parthood, location, or the like. Akiba (2000) has provided one such theory wherein indeterminate objects are modeled in terms of indeterminate coincidence (a precursor of the precisificational theories in Akiba 2004, 2014a, discussed in Section 3).[12]

Akiba starts off by assuming a plurality of concrete and precise worlds, along the lines of the pluriverse of Lewis (1986). But whereas the Lewisian picture takes worlds to be ways reality is not necessarily unactualized, Akiba takes them to be ways reality is not determinately unactualized. (In effect, nothing prevents worlds from playing both roles, as long the two roles are suitably distinguished.) And whereas on the former picture objects like persons, mountains, and electrons are world-bound, Akiba takes them to be *modal continuants* – that is, objects existing at multiple worlds. A modal continuant a exists at w by having some part at w. The maximal w-part of a, if any, is the mereological sum of a's w-parts. Thus, the proper name 'Isabelle Huppert' refers to a modal continuant, Isabelle Huppert, who has a maximal part at each world. (Let's suppose that every object has parts at all worlds.)[13]

Say objects *coincide* at w if their maximal w-parts are identical. Because objects are spread across worlds, they may coincide at some of them and not others. By virtue of being modal continuants, objects are determinately identical

---

[12] A similar theory is developed in Morreau (2002), where indeterminate objects are modeled in terms of indeterminate boundaries, compatibly with the conclusion of Evans's argument.

[13] Akiba's picture is analogous to *perdurantism* in the philosophy of time, except for times being replaced with worlds.

if they coincide at all worlds, otherwise they are determinately distinct. Statements of the form $\nabla(a = b)$ are therefore unsatisfiable, consistent with Evans's conclusion.

Nevertheless, Akiba makes room for indeterminate objects as follows:

AK. An object is said to be *indeterminate*$_{AK}$ if it coincides with a determinate object at some but not all worlds.

For example, Kilimanjaro is indeterminate$_{AK}$ insofar as it coincides with a determinate mountain-like k at some world, and with some other determinate mountain-like k' at another world.

Unlike the characterizations of object indeterminacy considered so far, AK defines 'indeterminate object' in terms of 'determinate object'. But what is a determinate object? It is one that coincides with a determinate object at all worlds, or at none – in other words, it is an object that is not indeterminate. Akiba (2000: 368) believes that the prospect of analyzing away both 'indeterminate' and 'determinate' at once are dim, and that the circularity should be broken by taking either term as unanalyzable.

It is of course legitimate to take a notion as primitive, especially when it plays a central role in metaphysical theorizing. One problem in the present context is that the relation *x coincides with y at some but not all worlds* is symmetric. Consider the scenario in Figure 2: are we supposed to regard A, B as determinate$_{AK}$, and C as indeterminate$_{AK}$, or the other way around? On Akiba's model, whereas facts about coincidence are an objective feature of the pluriverse, facts about determinacy and lack thereof are underdetermined, and any way to break the symmetry appears arbitrary. This suggests that the phenomenon of object indeterminacy is akin to contingent coincidence only up to a point, since in the modal case there appears to be no analog distinction between 'contingent' and 'noncontingent' objects.

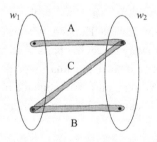

Figure 2 Coincident objects

3 States of Affairs

In Section 2, the question of metaphysical indeterminacy was addressed from a straightforward ontic standpoint, such that for reality to be indeterminate is for it to be populated with indeterminate objects. That strategy was motivated by the idea that the world is the totality of objects. We saw that, given fairly standard assumptions, object indeterminacy leads to indeterminate identities, which are ruled out by Evans's influential result. The latter may be resisted in a number of ways, some more promising than others, although at a significant cost in terms of either logical or metaphysical revisionism.

According to a different tradition, the world is the totality of states of affairs (Wittgenstein 1921; Turner, 2016; Rayo, 2017). On this view, the locus of worldly indeterminacy is not the object but the way the object is, viz., the state of affairs. The rationale for reorienting the discussion along such lines is fourfold.

First, we can reason by analogy with the phenomenon of semantic indeterminacy, which is not exhausted by the case of referential indeterminacy, but can also be located at the sentential level. Insofar as objects and states of affairs are the semantic values of referential terms and sentences, respectively, the present strategy follows a familiar pattern.

Second, Evans's argument has put considerable pressure on the advocates of indeterminate objects. Thus, if we want to explore the nature and possibility of metaphysical indeterminacy, it is methodologically wise to decouple it from talk of indeterminate objects, which is in fact what has happened in much of the recent literature.

Third, a number of putative examples of metaphysical indeterminacy involving the open future, indeterminate existence, quantum physics, and so forth are not reducible to object indeterminacy in any straightforward way, if at all. In order to accommodate such a broad spectrum of cases, it is advisable to go beyond the ontic approach.

Finally, it has probably not gone unnoticed that nearly every characterization of object indeterminacy discussed in Section 2 involves an indeterminacy sentential operator in its *definiens*, for example:

P. An object a is said to be *indeterminate$_P$* if there is something b such that it is indeterminate whether b is a part of a.

A full understanding of the spectrum of theories about object indeterminacy will therefore require that we formulate general truth conditions for statements of the form 'it is indeterminate whether p', and that 'indeterminate' is understood as capturing a worldly rather than merely semantic phenomenon.

3.1 From Semantic to Metaphysical Indeterminacy

Here is a popular and simple picture of the way competent speakers manage to describe the world. We mostly communicate by uttering (declarative) sentences: grammatically well-formed strings of words such as 'I am late for the 2:00 p.m. train' and 'Bob is bald'. Utterances take place in a context, which specifies a speaker, place, time, world, and so forth. An utterance is made true by a *state of affairs* (or simply *state*). For example, 'I am late for the 2:15 p.m. train' uttered by me at my place and time is made true by the state of Alessandro's being late for the train leaving the Milan Central Station at 2:15 p.m. CET. In natural language, states are referred to by terms obtained by nominalizing a sentence: from *a is so and so* to *a's being so and so*. I will follow the convention that [p] is the unique state of affairs (if any) picked out by nominalizing '*p*'.

A sentence in context is a *truthbearer*, and it expresses a set of states, namely the set of its *truthmakers* (Armstrong, 2004). For a state S to make a sentence false is for S to make its negation true. Thus, the state of grass' being grass green (i.e., Pantone 15-6437 TCX) is not only a truthmaker for 'grass is green', but also a falsemaker for 'grass is blue'. The notion at work here is that of *exact* truthmaker (Fine, 2017: 558). An exact truthmaker for '*p*' is a truthmaker for '*p*' that is wholly relevant to the truth of '*p*'. For example, grass' being grass green is an exact truthmaker for 'grass is green', whereas grass' being grass green and snow's being snow white (i.e., Pantone 11-0602 TPX) is not.

I will be making two substantive assumptions about the nature of truthmaking:

Necessitarianism. If S is a truthmaker for '*p*' then, necessarily, '*p*' is true if S obtains.

Maximalism. Necessarily, every truth has a truthmaker.

The truthmaking relation is many-many: a state can be a truthmaker for multiple sentences, and a sentence can be made true by multiple states.

States of affairs are finely individuated. The set of truthmakers for 'grass is green' is not identical with the set of truthmakers for 'grass is green and savory or grass is green and unsavory'. States are not too fine-grained, however. Since water is H_2O, the set of truthmakers for 'Laura drinks water' is identical with the set of truthmakers for 'Laura drinks H_2O'.

For many practical purposes, fine-grained content is a superfluous luxury. Suppose that states are partially ordered by a *containment* relation $\sqsubseteq$ such that $S \sqsubseteq Q$ iff Q entails S (iff, necessarily, Q obtains only if S obtains). For example:

[the teapot is made of gold] $\sqsubseteq$ [the teapot is smooth and made of gold]
[the teapot's top half is made of gold] $\sqsubseteq$ [the teapot is made of gold].

A *world* is a $\sqsubseteq$-maximal state, that is, a state that is not contained in any state other than itself. Call a world *actual* if it obtains. The following theses will be assumed throughout:

1. Necessarily, every state is contained in a world.
2. Necessarily, exactly one world obtains.

Let's say that 'p' is *true at* a world if this contains a truthmaker for 'p'. We identify *propositions* with sets of worlds, and the proposition expressed by 'p' with the set of worlds containing a truthmaker for 'p'. A proposition is said to obtain at world W just in case it has W as a member.

It follows that propositional content is coarse-grained: the proposition expressed by 'grass is green' is identical with the proposition expressed by 'grass is green and savory or grass is green and unsavory' – although not with the proposition expressed by 'grass is green or blue'. I will follow the convention that $\langle p \rangle$ is the proposition expressed by 'p'.

We identify *truth values* with sets of co-obtaining propositions. Thus, the truth value of 'grass is green' is identical with the truth value of 'grass is green or blue' – although not with the truth value of 'grass is blue'. True is the value assigned to a sentence that picks out some obtaining state, whereas False is the value assigned to a sentence whose negation picks out some obtaining state.

We say that the *semantic value* or *content* of a sentence is individuated hyperintensionally if it is a set of states of affairs, namely the set of its truth-makers; that it is individuated intensionally if it is a proposition; and that it is individuated extensionally if it is a truth value.

Indeterminacy is *semantic* when it originates at the interface of language and content. Let us assume a sparse, as opposed to abundant, conception of properties in such a way that, say, *being grass green* and *having mass of 3 kg* are properties, whereas *being grass green or snow white* and *having mass* are not. How exactly to characterize sparseness is far from trivial, but for present purpose, it will suffice to register that, on the sparse conception, not every predicate picks out a property.[14]

Suppose that there are such properties as *having 0 hairs, having at least 1 hair, . . . having at least 2,458 hairs, . . .* but no property of *being bald*. Insofar as ascriptions of properties to individuals are the semantic values of sentences, and assuming that semantic values are intensionally individuated, there will be such propositions as $\langle$Bob has 0 hairs$\rangle$, $\langle$Bob has at least 1 hair$\rangle$, . . . $\langle$Bob has at least 2,458 hairs$\rangle$. . ., but no such proposition as $\langle$Bob is bald$\rangle$. Thus, although an

---

[14] On sparseness, the *locus classicus* is Lewis (1983) (cf. Sider, 2011; Dorr & Hawthorne, 2013; Gómez Sánchez, 2023). I will return to the topic of sparseness in Section 3.4.

utterance of 'Bob is hairless' expresses ⟨Bob has 0 hairs⟩, there is no proposition expressed by 'Bob is bald', which raises the question of how to evaluate such sentences.

According to the standard account of semantic indeterminacy, *supervaluationism*, my uttering 'Bob is bald' could be assigned any one of a number of propositions each of which is not ruled out by the common usage of the predicate 'bald': ⟨Bob has 0 hairs⟩, ⟨Bob has at least 1 hair⟩, ... ⟨Bob has at least n hairs⟩, for some $n \geq 0$. If each of those propositions obtains, 'Bob is bald' is true; if each of them fails to obtain, 'Bob is bald' is false; if some obtains and some doesn't, 'Bob is bald' is indeterminate (Fine, 1975).[15] On the standard approach, then, indeterminacy arises when and only when a sentence has multiple candidate semantic values.

Since semantic indeterminacy is not the focus of this Element, it will be set aside unless noted otherwise. In passing, it is worth mentioning the metasemantic view that for 'Bob is bald' to be semantically indeterminate just is for it to be metaphysically indeterminate which of its candidate meanings is expressed by the sentence. On such a view, indeterminacy via supervaluations is metaphysical indeterminacy in disguise (cf. Merricks, 2001; Caie, 2014; Taylor & Burgess, 2015).

Metaphysical indeterminacy is indeterminacy that does not arise at the interface of language and content. The thesis may be stated in terms of the following *minimal condition*:

MIN. It is metaphysically indeterminate whether p iff it is indeterminate whether p, and 'p' has a determinate semantic value.

One might complain that the right-to-left direction of MIN is too demanding, in that it rules out the possibility of sentences in which semantic and metaphysical indeterminacy coexist (Barnes, 2010: 605). For example, we can suppose that 'Bob is bald' suffers from indeterminacy of the metaphysical variety because Bob is an indeterminate object, as well as indeterminacy of the semantic variety because 'bald' has no precise meaning. Then, goes the objection, 'Bob is bald' should be seen as expressing metaphysical indeterminacy, despite failing to have a determinate semantic value.

If statements of metaphysical indeterminacy can be semantically imprecise, how should they be evaluated? The natural route is to go supervaluationist: 'it is metaphysically indeterminate whether p' is true (false) just in case it is true (false) on all ways of making language perfectly precise. But

---

[15] If there is indeterminacy regarding the value of n, 'Bob is bald' will also be higher-order indeterminate.

this strategy might not give the desired results. If Williams (2008a) is right, semantic indeterminacy can originate in metaphysical indeterminacy. In such cases, we would only be able to make language perfectly precise by removing the underlying worldly imprecision. And once the latter is removed, the precisified statements of metaphysical indeterminacy will end up being false, thus making the original statement false, as well. Thus, it is by no means guaranteed that the supervaluationist scheme can help us make sense of a language in which the two kinds of indeterminacy are entangled. On the other hand, if semantic indeterminacy is never a result of worldly indeterminacy (cf. Section 2.4.2), we can restrict our attention to precise languages without any loss of generality.

Be that as it may, since semantic indeterminacy is at best a distraction in the present context, in what follows, I will focus on theories that satisfy MIN. Whether and how a language involving both sorts of indeterminacy can be made sense of, as well as spoken, remains an open problem.

It is worth observing that, on certain conditions, MIN entails a *de dicto-de re* link. In order to see that, we need to introduce a bit of extra machinery. By employing the letters $\mathbb{p}$, $\mathbb{q}$ ... as sentential variables, let us allow quantification into sentence position. We say that $\exists \mathbb{p}\phi$ is true given an assignment V of values to variables iff ϕ is true given an assignment V' differing from V at most on $\mathbb{p}$.

Given a logically higher-order language featuring an indeterminacy operator '∇', the following fact holds:

If 'p' has a determinate semantic value, then '∇p' is true only if '$\exists \mathbb{p}\nabla\mathbb{p}$' is true.

For suppose that '∇p' is true and that 'p' has a determinate semantic value s. Given an assignment mapping $\mathbb{p}$ to s, it follows that '$\nabla\mathbb{p}$' is true on that assignment. Hence, '$\exists \mathbb{p}\nabla\mathbb{p}$' is also true.

When '∇' is an operator of metaphysical indeterminacy, it is a straightforward consequence of the conjunction of MIN and the aforementioned fact that the following holds:

TEST. '∇p' is true only if '$\exists \mathbb{p}\nabla\mathbb{p}$' is true.

Plainly put, TEST tells us that, if it is metaphysically indeterminate whether so and so, then there is a way things could be such that it is indeterminate whether it obtains. Equivalently: if there is no fact of the matter whether p, then there is something about which there is no fact of the matter.

The remainder of Section 3 discusses a number of theories of metaphysical indeterminacy that meet the minimal condition, and that feature increasingly fine-grained conceptions of semantic content. A challenge to the minimal condition is considered in Section 3.4.

3.2 Extensional Theories

3.2.1 Many-Valued Logic

If the semantic values of sentences are identified with truth values, the best-known characterization of metaphysical indeterminacy involves *degrees of truth*. On one end of the spectrum, degree-theoretic (aka many-valued) semantics postulates three truth values: True, False, and Indeterminate (Tye, 1994) – or three truth-value statuses: true, false, and truth-valueless (Parsons, 2000). On the other end of the spectrum, degree-theoretic semantics involves continuum-many truth values, thus capturing the idea that the transition from definitely failing to ascribe a property to definitely ascribing it can be as gradual as is the transition from 0 to 1 on the real line (Machina, 1976).

For present purpose, we can restrict our attention to the case of a three-valued semantics, with values 1, 0.5, and 0 standing for True, Indeterminate and False, respectively. A notable example of three-valued semantics is Kleene's *strong logic of indeterminacy* whose valuations are defined as follows (Kleene, 1952):

$V(p) \in \{0, 0.5, 1\}$, if p is atomic

$V(\neg p) = 1 - V(p)$

$V(p \wedge q) = \min\{V(p), V(q)\}$

$V(p \vee q) = \max\{V(p), V(q)\}.$

The material conditional '$p \to q$' is defined as '$\neg p \vee q$', whereas the biconditional '$p \leftrightarrow q$' is defined as '$(p \wedge q) \vee (\neg p \wedge \neg q)$'. Although the logic can be naturally extended to predicate languages, I will set that case aside to avoid further complications.

Logical truth is truth on all valuations, and validity is truth preservation. Classical logic is obtained from Kleene's logic if only valuations with range $\{0, 1\}$ are considered. Kleene's logic makes room for the following characterization of metaphysical indeterminacy:

ExtGap. It is indeterminate whether p iff the truth value of 'p' is neither 1 nor 0.

So ExtGap equates indeterminacy to the existence of a truth-value gap. In order to express facts about (in)determinacy in the object language, we can introduce a sentential determinacy operator '**D**' by extending V so that $V(\mathbf{D}p) = 1$ if $V(p) = 1$, and $V(\mathbf{D}p) = 0$ otherwise. In that way, '**D**' satisfies the rule of **D**-introduction, thus licensing the inference from 'p' to '$\mathbf{D}p$'.

Kleene interpreted his theory epistemically, in such a way that 'it is indeterminate whether p' should be read as 'it is unknown whether p'. However, the theory warrants a stronger, realist interpretation. Since any sentence gets assigned a determinate truth value, whether 1, 0.5, or 0, the minimal condition MIN guarantees that ExtGap-indeterminacy is metaphysical in character. Moreover, once quantification into sentence position is allowed, it follows by TEST that many-valued logics license the inference from '∇p' to '$\exists p \nabla p$' (cf. Williamson, 2003a: 704). The result straightforwardly generalizes to any other many-valued logic of indeterminacy. Thus, Kleene's intended interpretation of the logic is a lie by omission. Sure, if there is no fact of the matter whether p, then it is unknowable whether p, and so it is unknown whether p. Lack of knowledge is merely a symptom of the underlying metaphysical indeterminacy.

Kleene's logic is nonclassical, in that it does not validate classical tautologies. For example, '$p \vee \neg p$' is indeterminate when 'p' is indeterminate. In fact, Kleene's semantics does not make any sentences logically true – it can at most make them logically not false. Dually, '$p \wedge \neg p$' is indeterminate if 'p' is. No sentence is logically false on Kleene's logic – it can at most be logically untrue.

Kleene's semantics is compositional in that, just like in the classical bivalent case, the truth value of a sentence is a function of the truth values of its subsentences. As we will see, this feature sets it apart from other approaches to metaphysical indeterminacy.

Both compositionality and nonclassicality are the source of a standard complain against Kleene's logic. Suppose that it is indeterminate whether Kilimanjaro is a particular mountain-shaped object k. On the present semantics, it is entailed that

Kilimanjaro is and is not k

is not false. But, goes the objection, both predicating and not predicating something of Kilimanjaro surely looks like an impossibility, no matter what the status of Kilimanjaro's identity happens to be. It is concluded that Kleene's semantics is formally inadequate. Similar considerations carry over to other many-valued logics.

Detractors of degree-theoretic semantics diagnose the problem by observing that connections between sentential truth values can be of two kinds. Sometimes, the connection is *truth-functional*: '$\neg p$' is false when 'p' is true; true when 'p' is false; indeterminate when 'p' is indeterminate. Sometimes, the connection is *penumbral*. The sentence 'Bob is or is not bald' is supposed to be true no matter what the truth value of 'Bob is bald' is; likewise for the falsity of 'Bob is and is not bald'. The case of classical tautologies and contradictions is a particular instance of a broader phenomenon. If Bob is hairier than John, and 'John is bald' is indeterminate, then 'Bob is bald' cannot be true. In this case too, the correct way of assigning truth values is no truth-functional matter. If these remarks are correct, the original sin of degree-theoretic semantics is that, by being compositional, it does not allow for penumbral connections (Fine, 1975: 270; Williamson, 1994: 135).   •

The advocate of degrees of truth can push back in a number of ways. First of all, it is helpful to address the special worry about classical tautologies and contradictions separately from the worry concerning penumbral connections at large. The general worry is raised in the context of vagueness – that is, indeterminacy involving sorites series, such as one that starts with the determinately bald, goes through the borderline bald, and ends with the determinately not bald. The standard view is that the phenomenon of vagueness results from semantic rather than metaphysical indeterminacy. Accordingly, the reason we are unable to draw a sharp line between the bald and the nonbald is that the extension of the predicate 'bald' is underspecified. The objection from penumbral connections is only relevant to the present discussion if vagueness is a worldly rather than semantic phenomenon, against the standard view. In fact, if vagueness is a consequence of semantic indeterminacy, there will not even be a property of baldness, and so no state of affairs of Bob's being bald. The standard view on vagueness therefore rules out that 'Bob is bald' has a determinate semantic value, which preempts the applicability of many-valued logics. Pace Williamson (2003a: 694), compositional treatments of metaphysical indeterminacy need not capture the penumbral connections between sentences about elements of a sorites series.

One might rejoin that even if the standard view is correct, and the phenomenon of vagueness lies outside the scope of a theory of metaphysical indeterminacy, degree-theoretic semantics should still be rejected insofar as they do not preserve classical tautologousness and contradictoriness. The complaint is typically raised on intuitive grounds. The reason 'Bob is and is not bald' is perceived as an impossibility is that (i) it is impossible for a sentence to be both true and false, and (ii) 'Bob is and is not bald' entails that 'Bob is bald' is both true and false. The complaint can be (and, in fact, usually is) dismissed by the friends of degrees of truth. Even by the lights of Kleene's logic it is the case that 'Bob is and is not bald' entails an impossibility. But entailment is truth preservation, which means that an impossibility is only derived if 'Bob is and is not bald' is true. Since on Kleene's logic a sentence of the form '$p \land \neg p$' can only be either false or indeterminate, the objection is easily defused.

3.2.2 Boolean Many-Valued Logic

One might still push back by arguing that classical logic should be retained not because our linguistic intuition says so, but out of theoretical conservatism. Logic is a theory and should be judged like one. Because classical logic is simple and powerful, and underlies mathematical reasoning, which in turn underlies all exact sciences, we may not want to throw it out unless as a last resort.

As Akiba (2017) has shown, one can have degrees of truth without relinquishing classical validities. In Kleene's many-valued logic, truth values are linearly ordered, which entails two things: that any two truth values can be compared; and that there is exactly one path from 0 to 1. On Akiba's *Boolean many-valued logic*, on the other hand, truth values form a Boolean algebra – that is, a set B (the values) endowed with operations $\sqcap$ (*meet*), $\sqcup$ (*join*) and $-$ (*complement*), as well as the distinguished elements 1 and 0, such that:

$$x \sqcap (x \sqcup y) = x$$

$$x \sqcup (x \sqcap y) = x$$

$$x \sqcup -x = 1$$

$$x \sqcap -x = 0.$$

The semantics is defined in terms of valuations from sentences to the domain B of some Boolean model such that:

$$A(p) \in B, \text{ if } p \text{ is atomic}$$

$$A(\neg p) = -A(p)$$

$$A(p \wedge q) = A(p) \sqcap A(q)$$

$$A(p \vee q) = A(p) \sqcup A(q).$$

The truth values in B are partially ordered by a relation $\leq$ such that $x \leq y := x \sqcap y = x$. (A strict partial order is defined as $x < y := x \leq y \wedge x \neq y$.) It follows that, in any Boolean model with more than two (and so at least four) values, two propositions may be incomparable with respect to their truth values; and that there exist multiple paths from 0 to 1.

A valuation A assigns 1 to '$p \vee \neg p$', as well as to every other classical tautology, and 0 to '$p \wedge \neg p$', as well as to every other classical contradiction. Once a suitable relation of logical consequence is defined (Akiba, 2017: 425), Boolean semantics can deal with sorites arguments in a similar way as standard degree-theoretic semantics.

Two issues nevertheless deserve attention. One has to do with comparatives involving indeterminate sentences. Let us say that, as far as adults go, someone who is 1 m tall is determinately not tall, and someone who is 2 m tall is determinately tall. Insofar as tallness comes in degrees, it will have borderline cases. Suppose that anyone between 1.45 m and 1.55 m is borderline tall. Laura, who is 1.55 m, is such that it is indeterminate whether she is tall. Yet, by being closer to 2 m than to 1 m, she is more tall than she is not. As it turns out, Boolean semantics can't do justice to that fairly straightforward conclusion. Since any value u other than 1 and 0 is such that it and its complement $-u$ lie on different paths of a Boolean model, every indeterminate sentence is incomparable with its negation. Therefore, it can't be the case that $-A$(Laura is tall) $< A$(Laura is tall), and so that A(Laura is not tall) $< A$(Laura is tall), as was just established.

Akiba (2022: 80) welcomes the result. If a proposition and its negation were always comparable, we could find a point of equilibrium in some possible individual, say Ana, who is just as tall as she is not tall, i.e., such that A(Ana is not tall) $= A$(Ana is tall). But then, concludes Akiba, Ana's size would represent a sharp cutoff between tallness and nontallness, thus ruling out indeterminacy about tallness.

Pace Akiba, however, a point of equilibrium need not be a cutoff point. Ana represents a cutoff between the tall and nontall just in case either Ana is tall and anyone shorter is not tall, or Ana is not tall and anyone taller is tall. Therefore, Ana represents a cutoff between the tall and nontall only if either she is tall or she is not tall. Crucially, that condition is not entailed by the fact that Ana is just as tall as she is not tall. In order to see that, consider the simpler case of Kleene's three-valued logic. If Ana is borderline tall, then she is a tallness point of equilibrium, since V(Ana is tall) $= 0.5 = 1 - V$(Ana is tall) $= V$(Ana is not tall). On the other hand, it is not the case that either Ana is tall or Ana is not tall, and so Ana does not represent a sharp cutoff between tallness and nontallness. The same consideration applies to Akiba's Boolean semantics, since by hypothesis the truth value of 'Ana is tall' is neither 1 nor 0.

The second issue with Boolean semantics concerns Akiba's own rationale for adopting it. Although he tells us that "Boolean valuations are immune to the problem of penumbral connections" (2022: 424), the theory is explicitly designed to address the special case of classical tautologies and contradictions, and does not accommodate penumbral connections of the nonlogical variety. Although the limitation need not worry the many-valued logician who regards vagueness as a semantic phenomenon, it should worry anyone who takes all indeterminacy to be metaphysical in character, such as Akiba (2014b) himself.

Be that as it may, Boolean semantics is an important example of a logic that is compositional yet able to preserve classical validities, pace Williamson and Fine. Adding further grist to the mill, Cobreros and colleagues (2013) defend a three-valued semantics that validates all logical truths and inference rules of classical logic – although not all classical metarules, such as the transitivity of entailment (if ϕ entails ψ, and ψ entails χ, then ϕ entails χ).

3.3 Intensional Theories

3.3.1 Indeterminate Propositions

Many-valued logics are gappy, in that they construe indeterminacy in terms of a third truth value (or truth-value status). The gappy strategy can be straightforwardly generalized from the extensional to the intensional case by taking sentential content to be a proposition rather than a truth value. Accordingly, every semantically precise sentence 'p' will partition logical space into three classes: the worlds at which it is true, or $\langle p \rangle$-worlds; the worlds at which it is false, or $\langle \neg p \rangle$-worlds; and the worlds at which it is neither true nor false. The picture makes room for a natural reading of indeterminacy in the world:

IntGap. It is indeterminate whether p iff the actual world is neither a $\langle p \rangle$-world nor a $\langle \neg p \rangle$-world.

As long as the background semantics maps each sentence 'p' to determinate semantic value $\langle p \rangle$, MIN guarantees that IntGap-indeterminacy is metaphysical. Accordingly, metaphysical indeterminacy will amount to a gap in logical space, that is to say, to the existence of some proposition $\langle p \rangle$ such that neither it nor its negation $\langle \neg p \rangle$ obtains (Figure 3).

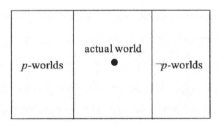

Figure 3 IntGap-indeterminacy

An instance of IntGap-indeterminacy is provided by quantum logic, which tells us that it is indeterminate whether, say, electron e has such and such spin whenever the actual state of the system does not select either the proposition ⟨electron e has such and such spin⟩ or the proposition ⟨electron e does not have such and such spin⟩. Unlike many-valued logic, quantum logic is noncompositional and validates some (although not all) classical tautologies. IntGap has been defended in the particular case of quantum indeterminacy in (Fletcher and Taylor, 2021a, 2021b; Torza, 2021, 2022; Lewis, 2022).

A hyperintensional formulation of quantum logic, and a discussion of its significance vis-à-vis indeterminacy is provided in Section 4. The remainder of Section 3.3 is devoted to intensional theories that are not wedded to any specific nonclassical logic.

3.3.2 Worlds: Concretism

We have been assuming that there is a plurality of ways the world can be, of which exactly one obtains, namely the actual one (Section 3.1). That stands in stark contrast to the view that every way the world can be obtains. A prominent reason for adopting a plurality of obtaining worlds is that it allows a reductive analysis of necessity and possibility talk (Lewis, 1986). But a middle ground view can also be adopted, namely that some although not all ways the world can be obtain. One might want to follow this route in order to attain a reductive analysis of (in)determinacy talk by analogy with the Lewisian strategy.

On such a view, each obtaining world is a way for reality to be precise. In other words, reality has not only a modal dimension, defined by the class of all worlds, but also a precisificational dimension, defined by the class of all obtaining worlds. While we say that 'necessarily p' is true just in case 'p' is true at all worlds, we say that 'determinately p' is true just in case 'p' is true at all obtaining worlds. This view is, like Lewis's, *concretist* insofar as it postulates a plurality of obtaining worlds. A concretist metaphysics of this sort is articulated and defended in Akiba (2004).

If multiple worlds obtain, which of them do we refer to when we speak of the actual world? Once again, we can take a page from Lewis. The modal realist regards 'actual' as an indexical: it refers to whichever happens to be the world of utterance. When one world is replaced by many, 'actual' will be semantically indeterminate: it refers to one of the obtaining worlds, although it is indeterminate which one.

Concretism makes room for an intensional characterization of metaphysical indeterminacy that does not postulate gaps in logical space. Let us assume that every semantically precise sentence partitions logical space into two classes: worlds at which it is true, and worlds at which it is false. Then,

IntConc1. It is indeterminate whether *p* iff there are both an obtaining ⟨*p*⟩-world and an obtaining ⟨¬*p*⟩-world.

Insofar as the background semantics assigns precise semantic values, MIN guarantees that IntConc1-indeterminacy is metaphysical in nature. (Note that the application of MIN is restricted to an object language that does not feature the semantically imprecise expression 'actually'.)

Metaphysical indeterminacy therefore arises just in case some proposition cuts across the class of obtaining worlds. For example, it will be metaphysically indeterminate whether Kilimanjaro is so and so just in case the class of obtaining worlds overlaps both ⟨Kilimanjaro is so and so⟩ and ⟨Kilimanjaro is not so and so⟩ (Figure 4).

Does the absence of gaps in logical space guarantee bivalence? First, we need to decide whether truth *simpliciter* amounts to (i) truth at all obtaining worlds or (ii) truth at the actual world. According to i, if it is metaphysically indeterminate whether *p*, then '*p*' will be neither true nor false, and vice versa. By adopting view ii, the truth value of a sentence '*p*' will depend on what is the case in actuality. As we said, if there are multiple obtaining worlds, it is indeterminate which of them is referred to as 'actual'. Consequently, if it is metaphysically indeterminate whether *p*, then '*p*' will be neither true nor false, and vice versa. Therefore, whether truth is understood via i or ii, bivalence is bound to fail on the present concretist theory. The absence of gaps in logical space does not suffice to guarantee a classical

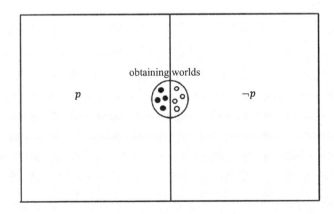

Figure 4 IntConc1-indeterminacy

semantics. It is worth noting on the other hand that, insofar as worlds are taken to be precise, concretism is compatible with classical logic.

The issue of bivalence is addressed in the revamped concretism of Akiba (2014a). The new theory, like its predecessor, postulates a precisificational dimension defined by the class of obtaining worlds, while ruling out the existence of gaps in logical space. The key new features are two. First, it is assumed that among the obtaining worlds there is a world $W_@$ designated as actual – presumably, the one we live in. Second, there is a binary accessibility relation on the set of worlds such that, informally, W is accessible from V just in case W does not determinately fail to obtain from V's perspective. Akiba takes accessibility to be reflexive and transitive.

Truth *simpliciter* is defined as follows:

'p' is true iff it is true at the actual world $W_@$.

Insofar as worlds are precise, bivalence holds. Moreover, the resulting semantics upholds compositionality: the truth value at a world of a molecular sentence is a function of the truth value of its constituents.

The accessibility relation defines a tree whose root is $W_@$, and whose leaves are the worlds accessible from $W_@$ that only access themselves. The associated notion of indeterminacy is as follows:

IntConc2. It is indeterminate whether p iff there are both a leaf $\langle p \rangle$-world and a leaf $\langle \neg p \rangle$-world.

Accordingly, metaphysical indeterminacy arises just when some proposition cuts across the leaf worlds. On the assumption that the assignment of semantic values to sentences is precise, MIN guarantees that IntConc2-indeterminacy is metaphysical.

Bivalence does not rule out indeterminacy, for whenever a sentence 'p' is true at $W_@$ but false at some leaf world, 'p' is going to be true, yet not determinately so. Thus, with a modicum of extra structure, revamped concretism attains the semantic conservatism that had escaped its predecessor.

Do IntConc1 and IntConc2 produce a reductive analysis of indeterminacy? The former does, since its truth conditions for statements of the form 'it is indeterminate whether p' only involve first-order quantification over obtaining worlds, as well as categorical facts about what goes on at each of those worlds. In this respect, IntConc1 is analogous to Lewisian realism. IntConc2 does not, however, since it is stated in terms of a primitive accessibility relation specifying which worlds do not determinately fail to obtain from any given world's viewpoint. By failing to analyze away indeterminacy, IntConc2 fails to produce what is arguably the main theoretical advantage of its concretist predecessor.

Both concretist strategies inherit many of the difficulties of Lewisian modal realism. I will mention just two. First, they are bound to face the notorious 'incredulous stare' of those who think that the theoretical benefit of concretism can hardly offset its seemingly preposterous ontological demands. In the specific case of Akiba's proposal, one might complain that, if our best shot at making sense of metaphysical indeterminacy commits us to a plurality of obtaining worlds, so much the worse for metaphysical indeterminacy. Although the incredulous stare is hardly a demonstrative move, it signals that the theory at issue might be guilty of intellectual hubris.

The second point is a variation on an objection that Williamson (2013: ch. 1.4) has raised against Lewis's modal realism. When philosophers say things like 'there are numbers', or 'there are no disembodied spirits', they intend to state a thesis about what there is unrestrictedly.[16] The same intention is retained if existential statements are embedded in modal operators. For example, by saying 'there can be no disembodied spirits', we mean that there is no possible interpretation of the quantifier that ranges over disembodied spirits. However, by saying 'there can be no disembodied spirits', the modal realist is stating that there is no way of restricting the actual interpretation of the quantifier to some world or other so that it ranges over disembodied spirits. The modal realist's paraphrase fails to respect the intended reading of the quantifier as being unrestricted.

The objection carries over to concretist theories of indeterminacy. By 'it is indeterminate whether there is something composed of a and b', we mean to interpret the quantifier unrestrictedly, even if it is in the scope of an indeterminacy operator. However, such an interpretation is ruled out if the indeterminacy operator is understood by analogy with Lewis's modal realism.

3.3.3 Worlds: Ersatzism

One need not commit to a plurality of obtaining worlds in order to reap the benefits that possible worlds have to offer (with one notable caveat to which we will return shortly). All we need is for some property to define the set of worlds playing the precisificational role. If the property of obtaining cannot do so, some other will have to take its place.

Let us start by assuming that there are no gaps in logical space: every proposition is such that either it or its negation obtains. Also, suppose that our

---

[16] In effect, the very possibility of quantifying over absolutely everything is controversial, although the issue will have to be set aside. See Williamson (2003b) for a defense of unrestricted quantification.

metatheory features the primitive expression 'it is determinate that'. The relevant class of worlds can then be defined as follows:

A world is an *ersatz actuality* iff it is not determinate that it fails to obtain.

On the present view, although there is just one maximal state of affairs that obtains, namely the actual world, there may be multiple maximal states of affairs that do not determinately fail to obtain. The relevant notion of indeterminacy can now be defined thus:

IntErsatz. It is metaphysically indeterminate whether p iff there are both a $\langle p \rangle$-ersatz actuality and a $\langle \neg p \rangle$-ersatz actuality.

That IntErsatz-indeterminacy is metaphysical is guaranteed by the minimal condition MIN, provided that the background semantics determinately maps each sentence 'p' to the proposition $\langle p \rangle$. Metaphysical indeterminacy therefore arises just in case some proposition cuts across the class of ersatz actualities. For it to be metaphysically indeterminate whether Kilimanjaro is so and so, the proposition $\langle$Kilimanjaro is so and so$\rangle$ will have to obtain at some ersatz actuality and fail to obtain at some other.

This construal of indeterminacy finds its most mature formulation in Barnes and Williams (2011), a 'worldly' version of the nonstandard supervaluationist account of semantic indeterminacy articulated in McGee and McLaughlin (1994). (Applications and variants of the view are also found in Barnes & Cameron, 2008; Barnes & Williams, 2009; Barnes, 2010; Darby & Pickup, 2021; Mariani, Michels & Torrengo, 2021).

IntErsatz allows us to formulate a precisificational account of the target phenomenon without committing to a plurality of concrete worlds. The gain is not free of charge, however. As Quine would put it, the ersatzist strategy offers an improvement in ontology paid for in the coin of ideology. By mirroring Lewis's reductive analysis of modal talk, the concretism of Akiba (2004) was able to offer a reductive analysis of (in)determinacy talk: truth conditions for statements of the form 'it is indeterminate whether p' only involve first-order quantification over obtaining worlds, as well as categorical facts about what goes on at each of those worlds. On the other hand, on the ersatzist strategy, the precisifications are not worlds that obtain, but worlds that do not determinately fail to obtain. Since stating that condition requires the very notion of (in)determinacy, IntErsatz fails to yield a reductive analysis.

Whether an increase in ontological parsimony is worth both a decrease in ideological parsimony and the loss of conceptual analysis can be assessed only on the basis of broader considerations about theory choice in metaphysics. On this point, it has been argued that a theory's ideology is not merely a choice of concepts devoid of any metaphysical import (Sider, 2011; Finocchiaro, 2019). On the contrary, if accepting the truth of a theory that entails 'there are numbers' will commit one to the mind-independent existence of numbers, likewise accepting the truth of a theory cast in modal terms will commit one to mind-independent modal structure. Consequently, adopting a theory with a primitive (in)determinacy operator will bear on the resulting picture of reality one accepts, namely a world endowed with precisificational structure.

Does bivalence hold on the ersatz world approach? It depends on how truth *simpliciter* is construed. If it amounts to truth at all ersatz actualities, bivalence clearly fails. If on the other hand, it amounts to truth at the actual world, bivalence holds, since worlds are precise by hypothesis. Advocates of the ersatz approach to indeterminacy typically choose the latter option in order to avoid semantic revisionism. As I argue in the following subsections, however, it is far from clear that retaining bivalence in the face of indeterminacy is desirable.

Since worlds are precise, the ersatz world account of indeterminacy is compatible with classical logic. Indeed, the formulation in Barnes and Williams (2011) provides a model theory that validates all truths and inference rules of classical logic. Furthermore, if truth is defined as truth at the actual world, the semantics of ersatz supervaluationism upholds compositionality.

The combination of bivalence, classicality, and compositionality is advertised as a key feature by the advocates of the ersatz world approach, in that it shows that making sense of metaphysical indeterminacy does not require any logical or semantic revisionism. However, the way logical and semantic conservatism is attained drives a wedge between truth and determinate truth, as witnessed by the fate of **D**-introduction.

Let us consider the point in the ersatz case, although the concretist version can be stated *mutatis mutandis*. Say that '**D**p' is true if 'p' is true at all ersatz actualities, and suppose that it is indeterminate whether p. Because bivalence holds, 'p' is either true or false. If it is true, then '$p \land \neg \mathbf{D}p$' is true; if it is false, then '$\neg p \land \neg \mathbf{D}\neg p$' is true. Either way, its being the case that p does not suffice for its being determinately the case that p. As I am going to argue, the existence of a gap between truth and determinate truth leads to a number of problems.

3.3.4 Against Bivalence: Symmetry

Let us focus on a particular class of indeterminacy scenarios that, for lack of a better term, I will refer to as *symmetric*. An instance of indeterminacy is symmetric when, by the precisificational lights, all ways of making it precise are on a par in all relevant respects. An example of symmetric scenario is the one of Anne the amoeba that splits into two daughter cells, Betty and Claire, which are intrinsically indistinguishable, equally distant from Anne, and so forth. By saying that it is indeterminate whether Anne survives as Betty rather than Claire, we are therefore imagining a symmetric situation wherein each daughter cell has equal right to being identified with the mother. Of course, there are scenarios of indeterminacy that are not symmetric, namely when some ways of making things precise are more salient than others – for instance, if either daughter cell is more similar to the mother in terms of shape, size, and so forth. Such asymmetric scenarios can be set aside for present purpose.

Now, suppose that it is indeterminate whether Kilimanjaro is one of a number of precise mountain-like objects, and that the scenario is symmetric. For simplicity's sake, we can assume that k and k' are the only candidate precisifications. According to the ersatz world account, there is an ersatz actuality at which $\langle$Kilimanjaro is $k\rangle$ obtains, as well as an ersatz actuality at which $\langle$Kilimanjaro is $k'\rangle$ obtains. This condition intends to capture the thesis that, for each of the things that Kilimanjaro might be, there is a way the world can be such that Kilimanjaro is just that way.

So far, so good. Recall now that, among the ersatz actualities, there is exactly one that obtains. Thus, either $\langle$Kilimanjaro is $k\rangle$ obtains and $\langle$Kilimanjaro is $k'\rangle$ does not, or vice versa. So

(a) Either 'Kilimanjaro is k' is true and 'Kilimanjaro is k'' is false, or vice versa.

This fact does not square well with the hypothesis that the scenario is symmetric. For what makes k and k' equal candidates, if not the fact that the world makes 'Kilimanjaro is k' neither more nor less true than 'Kilimanjaro is k''? In other words, symmetry demands that

(b) 'Kilimanjaro is k' and 'Kilimanjaro is k'' have equal truth value.

By entailing (a), the ersatz world account undermines the symmetry encoded in (b). The moral is that the account is able to preserve bivalence on pain of severing the connection between

It is indeterminate whether p or q

and

'p' is neither more nor less true than 'q'

in all symmetric scenarios. The argument applies *mutatis mutandis* to the bivalent concretism of Akiba (2014a).

Supervaluationists could reply by pointing to an analogy between indeterminacy and contingency. John von Neumann grew up in Budapest. He could have lived on either the western side (Buda) or the eastern side (Pest) of the Danube River. Thus, it is contingent whether he grew up in Buda or Pest. As a matter of fact, he grew up in Pest. What we have here is a symmetric scenario involving contingency, alongside an asymmetry as to which relevant possibility is actualized. Likewise, we may have a symmetric scenario involving indeterminacy, alongside an asymmetry as to what is true. The familiarity of the modal case, goes the reply, can help us get a better grip on the supervaluationist picture.

The problem with this line of resistance is that the analogy between indeterminacy and truth, on the one hand, and contingency and actuality, on the other, is flawed. For there is no such a thing as a class of symmetric modal scenarios such that the truth of

It is contingent whether p or q

requires the truth of

'p' is neither more nor less actual than 'q'.

In fact, there is even linguistic evidence for the disanalogy. For in the modal case, we can say not only that

It is contingent whether JvN grew up in Buda rather than Pest

but also that

It is contingent that JvN grew up in Buda rather than Pest

thus signaling which relevant possibility is actualized, namely that JvN grew up in Buda. On the other hand, we can say

It is indeterminate whether Kilimanjaro is k rather than k'

but we would never say

*It is indeterminate that Kilimanjaro is k rather than k'

in order to signal that, indeterminacy notwithstanding, Kilimanjaro is k.[17]

---

[17] Of course, in some cases 'it is indeterminate that. . . ' is admissible, namely when it is used as a synonym of 'it is not determinate that. . . ' – that is, as the negation of 'it is determinate that. . . '. But that use is not a factive version of 'it is indeterminate whether. . . ', standardly defined as 'it is not determinate that. . . and it is not determinate that not. . . ', and so it is not a counterpart of the factive 'it is contingent that. . . '.

3.3.5 Against Bivalence: Skepticism

Williamson (1994) has recommended an *epistemicist* solution to the paradoxes of vagueness. On his view, vagueness does not arise from indeterminacy, whether semantic or metaphysical. An utterance of 'Bob is bald' expresses a proposition ascribing a precise upper bound to the number (or density) of hairs on Bob's scalp; and that proposition either obtains or fails to obtain. What makes it vague whether Bob is bald, says Williamson, is that we are in principle unable to identify the proposition expressed by 'Bob is bald'.

Perhaps the main selling point of the epistemicist strategy is that it deals with the sorites, as well as other vagueness-related phenomena, without any semantic or logical revisionism. Nevertheless, Williamson's view is usually met with skepticism, since it asks us to accept that predicates such as 'bald' and 'tall' have precise meanings. In other words, the epistemicist is committed to the existence of brute semantic facts – brute because there is no explanation as to why 'Bob is bald' means, say, ⟨Bob has at most 2,453 hairs⟩ rather than ⟨Bob has at most 2,454 hairs⟩. Although any theory is one way or another bound to rest on unexplained facts of some sort, the epistemicist strategy appears to rest on the wrong sort of unexplained facts, which is what makes it so hard to believe (Keefe, 2000: 64). This complaint, despite its intuitive and therefore nondemonstrative nature, is so pervasive that it has relegated epistemicism to the status of fringe view.

The very same kind of skepticism can be aimed at the bivalent precisificational accounts of metaphysical indeterminacy discussed in Sections 3.3.2–3.3.3, which take it to be a brute fact that, say, either 'Kilimanjaro is k' is true or 'Kilimanjaro is k'' is true, even when it is indeterminate which. On the one hand, those accounts accept the pretheoretical datum that we are not justified in identifying Kilimanjaro with any precise object; on the other hand, they postulate the existence of a correct, if mysterious and unknowable way of identifying Kilimanjaro with a precise object. Although this posit grants them the semantic conservatism they seek, it introduces brute facts at a juncture where it is hard to believe that any could be found. Indeed, in this respect, the key difference between epistemicism and the precisificational views is that the former posits brute facts at the language–world interface, whereas the latter posits them in the precisificational structure of reality.

3.3.6 Against Bivalence: No Fact of the Matter

Barnes and Williams (2011) take metaphysical indeterminacy to be a kind of indeterminacy. Indeed, they defend the intelligibility of metaphysical indeterminacy by arguing that, if we can understand indeterminacy *simpliciter*, we can also understand indeterminacy with a worldly source – although see Eklund (2011) for criticism.

But is bivalence compatible with indeterminacy? As remarked in Section 1.1, it is common among philosophers to use interchangeably the expressions 'it is indeterminate' and 'there is no fact of the matter' (cf. Taylor, 2018: fn. 17). Precisificational theories of indeterminacy are motivated along the same lines: "The guiding idea here is that there is no fact of the matter which one of the ersatz worlds of the intended model is in fact the actualized one" (Barnes & Williams, 2011: 125).

To be sure, it is nearly analytic that it is indeterminate whether p only if there is no fact of the matter whether p. That conditional indeed helps explain why epistemicism provides an indeterminacy-free account of vagueness: it is either true or false that Bob is bald; so, there is a fact of the matter whether Bob is bald; therefore, it is determinate whether Bob is bald.

The same line of thought applies to the ersatz-world account of indeterminacy: (i) it is either true or false that Kilimanjaro is k; so, (ii) there is a fact of the matter whether Kilimanjaro is k; consequently, (iii) it is determinate whether Kilimanjaro is k. It must be concluded that ersatz-world indeterminacy is not indeterminacy, after all. The moral also applies to the concretism of Akiba (2014a).

Advocates of bivalent semantics could backtrack and reply in one of two ways. They may reject the inference from i to ii, by claiming that ii only follows from 'it is either determinately true or determinately false that Kilimanjaro is k'. Alternatively, they may reject the inference from ii to iii, by claiming that iii only follows from 'there is a determinate fact of the matter whether Kilimanjaro is k'. Either way, the advocates of ersatz supervaluationism would also have to reject the analogous inferences in the epistemicist case, which would leave them hard-pressed to explain in what sense Williamson provides an indeterminacy-free account of vagueness, a point explicitly endorsed in Barnes and Williams (2011: 106).

3.4 *De re* Indeterminacy and Sparseness

We have been exploring the view that the locus of metaphysical indeterminacy is sentential content, and we have done so by assuming that statements of metaphysical indeterminacy are semantically precise, as per the minimal condition (MIN) introduced in Section 3.1.

Since most of the intensional views that have been discussed are precisificational (IntConc1, IntConc2, IntErsatz), it may come as a surprise that there is an argument purporting to show that the following three conditions are jointly inconsistent (Williamson, 2003a: 701):

a. It is metaphysically indeterminate whether p;
b. MIN;
c. Metaphysical indeterminacy is modeled in precisificational terms.

To fully appreciate the gist of the argument, it will be helpful – although not strictly necessary – to formulate it for a predicate, rather than a sentential language. This involves generalizing MIN, as well as TEST, to second-order predicate languages:

MIN*. It is metaphysically indeterminate whether Pa iff it is indeterminate whether Pa, and both 'P' and 'a' have determinate semantic values.

When '∇' is an operator of metaphysical indeterminacy, and higher-order quantification is allowed, then

TEST*. '∇Pa' is true only if '$\exists x \exists X \nabla X x$' is true.
(The proof of TEST* mirrors the proof of TEST.)

In order for the argument to have the desired generality, we need a notion of precisification that abstracts away from the particular metaphysical choices. Accordingly, let us define a precisification I model-theoretically as an interpretation of the nonlogical vocabulary, together with rules for assigning the value True or False at I to each formula given an assignment of values to the variables.
    Now, suppose that

∇Pa

is true and expresses an instance of metaphysical indeterminacy. (On the present semantics, '∇Pa' is true just in case there is a precisification I such that the value of 'a' at I is a member of the extension of 'P' at I, and there is a precisification J such that the value of 'a' at J is not a member of the extension of 'P' at J.) Given MIN* and TEST*, it follows from '∇Pa' that

$\exists x \exists X \nabla X x$

which is true just in case there is a valuation V such that $V(x)$ is a member of $V(X)$ at some but not all precisifications. Here is the crucial bit: the value assigned to a variable is not a function of a precisification – unlike the semantic value of a nonlogical constant, like 'P' or 'a', which can vary across precisifications. So, given a valuation V, 'Xx' is either true on all precisifications, or false on all precisifications, which makes '$\exists x \exists X \nabla X x$' unsatisfiable. Hence, a, b, and c are jointly inconsistent. QED.
    The argument might be seen as evidence for an intensional reformulation of variable assignments. On this more liberal semantics, the value of a first-order

variable is not an individual, but an intensional individual (i.e., a function from precisifications to individuals); and the value of a second-order variable is not a set, but an intensional set (i.e., a function from precisifications to sets). Accordingly, it will no longer be the case that 'Xx' is either true on all precisifications or false on all precisifications, thus making room for *de re* indeterminacy.

A potential problem with adopting an ontology of intensional individuals and sets is that all indeterminacy will trivially turn out to be metaphysical. For suppose that it is indeterminate whether Pa – leaving it open whether that is so in virtue of language or reality. As long as the universe of discourse is unrestricted, it will contain all possible intensional individuals. Therefore, there is going to be a function that, at every precisification I, picks out the referent of 'a' at I. Likewise, there is going to be a function that, at every precisification I, picks out the set that is the extension of 'P' at I. In short, both 'P' and 'a' have determinate semantic values. It follows, by MIN*, that it is metaphysically indeterminate whether Pa.

The objection to the adoption of intensional entities can be resisted as follows. By allowing the second-order quantifier to range over all functions from precisifications to sets, we were presupposing an ontology of abundant properties. One may want to adopt a sparse ontology instead. Accordingly, most intensional sets are just too gerrymandered to deserve the title of property and, therefore, will not be elements of the domain of discourse. Once the domain is suitably restricted, it will no longer be trivially the case that 'P' has a determinate semantic value. (The same observation carries over to 'a' by adopting an ontology of sparse intensional individuals.[18])

A potential complaint is that, by assuming a sparse ontology of properties, the resulting notion of indeterminacy will be saddled with a controversial metaphysical posit, and therefore lack the desired generality. Notice, however, that the very same complaint could be raised against any view that does not regard all indeterminacy as metaphysical. For the indeterminacy of 'Bob is bald' can originate either in language or in the world (Section 3.1). If there is no baldness property, the sentence will lack a precise semantic value, and the indeterminacy will as a result be linguistic. If there is a baldness property, on the other hand, there is also the proposition that Bob is bald (provided that 'Bob' is referentially determinate), and so 'Bob is bald' will be metaphysically indeterminate. Unless the underlying ontology of properties is sparse, all indeterminacy is bound to be metaphysical, whether or not it is modeled precisificationally. And because many advocates of metaphysical indeterminacy are pluralists, and so acknowledge the

---

[18] For a generalization of naturalness to the semantic values of first-order variables, as well as vocabulary of any logical type, see Sider (2011).

existence of semantic indeterminacy, the assumption of sparseness happens to be widely shared, if unstated. To conclude, conditions a, b, and c can be reconciled given a metaphysics of sparse properties, which is arguably indispensable on independent grounds.

3.5 Hyperintensional Theories

3.5.1 Explanation

According to the hyperintensional, aka fine-grained account of sentential content, the semantic value of a sentence is a set of states of affairs, namely the set of its truthmakers. On this account, metaphysical indeterminacy will have to involve some funny business at the level of truthmakers (world) rather than the truthmaking relation (semantics).

Before delving into any specific theory, let us consider why the hyperintensional approach is more helpful in shedding light on the nature of indeterminacy. The role meanings play is not the same in formal semantics and in metaphysics. The formal semanticist's job is descriptive – it is to provide models of (a fragment of) natural language in a way that allows us to assign the expected truth values, as well as account for the speakers' inferential patterns. In order to model on what conditions 'p' is true, it will suffice to assign 'p' a proposition that obtains at a world just in case 'p' is true at that world. For such a task, intensions are, in most instances, good enough.

The metaphysician's job, on the other hand, is often explanatory: it is not exhausted by stating on what conditions a sentence is true (false), but it also aims to establish why it is true (false). The fact that the proposition ⟨snow is white or green⟩ obtains is necessary and sufficient for 'snow is white or green' to be true, yet it falls short of telling us what makes the sentence true. The obtaining of [snow is Pantone 11-0602 TPX], on the other hand, goes a long way toward explaining why 'snow is white or green' happens to have the truth value that it has. Likewise, the falsity of 'the laptop weighs 3 kg' is hardly explained by the obtaining of ⟨the laptop does not weigh 3 kg⟩, although it is explained by the obtaining of [the laptop weighs 1 kg]. One way to put the matter is that hyperintensional semantics is, unlike its intensional counterpart, sensitive to the source of a sentence's truth value status.

This observation about explaining truth and falsehood carries over to the task of explaining indeterminacy. Consider the case of quantum mechanics (cf. sec. 4). For each spatial direction $x, y, z \ldots$ in which a particle's spin can be measured, there exists a corresponding property of x-spin, y-spin, z-spin $\ldots$ According to orthodox quantum mechanics, there are pairs of spin properties along different directions that are *complementary* in that they cannot both have determinate values for a given system at the same time. If x-spin and y-spin are one such pair, it follows that whenever an electron has y-spin up, there is no fact of the matter whether it has x-spin up or x-spin down.

Now, the obtaining of ⟨it is indeterminate whether the electron has x-spin up⟩, though necessary and sufficient for 'the electron has x-spin up' to be indeterminate, does not tell us what makes that sentence indeterminate. Again, intensions do not play the desired explanatory role. Admittedly, the intensional theories discussed in Section 3.3 fare somewhat better in that they provide more nuanced indeterminacy conditions. For example, IntGap tells us that 'the electron has x-spin up' is indeterminate iff neither ⟨the electron has x-spin up⟩ nor ⟨the electron does not have x-spin up⟩ obtains; whereas IntErsatz tells us that the sentence is indeterminate just in case ⟨the electron has x-spin up⟩ obtains at some ersatz actuality, and ⟨the electron does not have x-spin up⟩ obtains at some other ersatz actuality.

But we can do better. In the quantum-mechanical case at hand, the indeterminacy of 'the electron has x-spin up' happens to be fully explained by the obtaining of the state of affairs [the electron has y-spin up]. Indeed, the electron's being y-spin up is incompatible both with the obtaining of a truthmaker for 'the electron has x-spin up', namely [the electron has x-spin up], and with the obtaining of a falsemaker for 'the electron has x-spin up', namely [the electron has x-spin down].

To sum up, a semantics formulated in terms of fine-grained, rather than coarse-grained content could in principle help us formulate a theory of indeterminacy that is explanatorily superior to the proposals considered so far. While keeping that point in mind, let us consider hyperintensional approaches to metaphysical indeterminacy.

3.5.2 Truthmaker Indeterminacy

A plurality of objects a, b, c ... is said to *compose* a further object d if d is the smallest object having a, b, c ... as parts. When it comes to material objects, a classical problem in the metaphysics literature is the *special composition question* (van Inwagen, 1987):

SCQ. When does composition occur?

A number of answers have been defended. At one end of the spectrum is the nihilist solution: composition never occurs. On this view, mereological atoms are all there is. So neither you nor I exist, nor do physical atoms or galaxies. At the other end of the spectrum is the universalist solution: composition always occurs. According to universalism, which is upheld by classical mereology, you and I exist, as well as the sum of you and I, and the sum of your left ear and some remote galaxy. Then there are all sorts of restrictionist views, which take composition to occur in some but not all cases. One might think, for example, that things compose a further thing just in case they are fastened together, or they are physically connected, or – as van Inwagen (1990) notoriously argued – their joint activities constitute a life. What is interesting about such restrictions, and countless many others, is that they are imprecise, thus making the composition relation indeterminate.

Composition can be either semantically or metaphysically indeterminate, depending on how it is restricted. One might say that (i) things compose a further thing iff they are close enough. Since 'close enough' is semantically indeterminate, the resulting view entails that in some cases it is going to be semantically indeterminate whether composition takes place.

Now, say that (ii) things compose a further thing iff their average pairwise distance is less than some constant ε. We may think of ii as a result of precisifying 'close enough' in i. Thus, if there is any indeterminacy in composition arising from such an answer to the special composition question, it will be metaphysical in character.

Consider a scenario consisting of two microphysical particles a and b, where a has a determinate position value x, whereas b has a determinate momentum value p. The quantum-mechanical properties of position and momentum are complementary, in that having determinate position rules out having determinate momentum, and vice versa. So b has no determinate position value. Let us suppose that the region where b might be found includes some point whose distance from a is less than ε, as well as some point whose distance from a is greater than ε (Figure 5). It is therefore indeterminate whether the distance between a and b is less than ε, and so, by condition ii, whether a and b compose something. Since the reasoning does not employ any semantically vague language, it must be concluded (via MIN) that we are dealing with an instance of metaphysically indeterminate composition.

Here is a way to make sense of the present scenario in hyperintensional terms. First, assume that states are closed under composition: fusions of states are states.[19] Assume also that, when a plurality $S, T, Q \ldots$ of states composes a further state U, the latter determinately obtains iff each of $S, T, Q \ldots$ determinately obtains; and it determinately fails to obtain iff one of $S, T, Q \ldots$ determinately fails to obtain.

Given ii, the fusion of a pair of states of the form

[a is located at x], [b is located at x']

---

[19] Insofar as states are not material objects, the fact that universalism holds for the former is compatible with its failing for the latter.

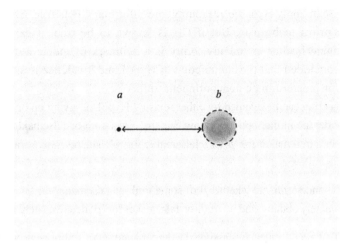

Figure 5 Indeterminate distance

is a truthmaker for 'a and b compose something' if the distance between x and x' lies strictly between 0 and ε, and it is a falsemaker otherwise. Since in the scenario at hand there is no x' such that [b is located at x'] determinately obtains, no truthmaker for 'a and b compose something' determinately obtains. Moreover, since there are x and x' such that [a is located at x] determinately obtains, and [b is located at x'] indeterminately obtains, the fusion of any two such states is a truthmaker for 'a and b compose something' that indeterminately obtains.

Generalizing away, we get the following view Barnes (2010: 609):

Hype1. It is indeterminate whether p iff some truthmaker for 'p' indeterminately obtains, and no truthmaker for 'p' determinately obtains.

Insofar as Hype1 is formulated against the backdrop of a precise semantics, MIN guarantees that Hype1-indeterminacy is metaphysical in character.

Given Hype1, indeterminacy is compatible with bivalence. For, as long as the metatheory does not license the inference from 'S obtains' to 'S determinately obtains', a sentence can have an obtaining truthmaker but no determinately obtaining truthmaker. Hence, it can be true that p, yet metaphysically indeterminate whether p.

Here is an objection to the conjunction of Hype1 and bivalence. Pick any indeterminate noncontingent truth, such as the continuum hypothesis (CH) – the thesis that the cardinality of the reals is the smallest uncountable cardinal. The CH is either true of false. If it is false, it is so by necessity. It will then have no truthmaker, and a fortiori no indeterminately obtaining truthmaker. So CH will not be indeterminate. Contradiction. Because bivalence holds, we can apply *reductio* reasoning and infer that CH is true. So CH is known a priori to be true. But if CH is known to be true, it cannot be indeterminate insofar as unknowability is a hallmark of indeterminacy. It must be concluded that the conjunction of Hype1 and bivalence is unable to account for indeterminate noncontingent truth.

The objection can be avoided by either revising Hype1 or giving up bivalence. Let's consider the former option for now. Say that S is a truth-or-falsemaker for 'p' if it is either a truthmaker for 'p' or a falsemaker for 'p'. The revised characterization goes as follows:

Hype2. It is indeterminate whether p iff some truth-or-falsemaker for 'p' indeterminately obtains, and no truth-or-falsemaker for 'p' determinately obtains.

Provided that every sentence is assigned a determinate set of truth-or-falsemakers, MIN guarantees that Hype2-indeterminacy is metaphysical in nature.

Now, CH may be necessarily false, and so have no indeterminately obtaining truthmakers, yet have some indeterminately obtaining truth-or-falsemaker. Thus, Hype2 avoids the objection to Hype1 while retaining bivalence.

3.5.3 Truthmaker Gaps

Insofar as the objections to bivalent intensional theories from Sections 3.3.4–3.3.6 can be repurposed in a hyperintensional setting, one may want to tackle the objection to Hype1 by giving up bivalence instead. Once the distinction between obtaining and determinately obtaining is collapsed, Hype2 gives way to a significantly simpler solution:

HypeGap1. It is indeterminate whether p iff no truth-or-falsemaker for 'p' obtains.

Provided that every sentence has a determinate set of truth-or-falsemakers, MIN guarantees that HypeGap1-indeterminacy is metaphysical.

Our running example involving indeterminate composition should now be understood as follows. Take the fusion F of a pair of states [a is located at x], [b is located at x'].

F makes 'a and b compose something' true if the distance between x and x' lies strictly between 0 and ε; it makes it false otherwise. Moreover, suppose that F obtains iff each of its components obtains. Insofar as b has determinate momentum, it has no determinate position, hence there is no x' such that [b is located at x'] obtains. So, no truth-or-falsemaker for 'a and b compose something' obtains. It follows by HypeGap1 that it is metaphysically indeterminate whether a and b compose something.

3.5.4 Indeterminate-Makers

Recall the rationale for adopting a fine-grained notion of semantic content: it provides a way to specify what makes a sentence true, false, or indeterminate – and not just when it is true, false, or indeterminate. For example, it allows us to say that 'the electron has x-spin up' is made true by the obtaining of [the electron has x-spin up], false by the obtaining of [the electron has x-spin down], and indeterminate by the obtaining of, for example, [the electron has y-spin up].

Surprisingly, none of the fine-grained notions of indeterminacy considered so far are able to fulfill that promise. Hype1 (as well as Hype2) tells us that 'the electron has x-spin up' is indeterminate partly because [the electron has x-spin up] indeterminately obtains. HypeGap1 tells us that 'the electron has x-spin up' is indeterminate because neither [the electron has x-spin up] nor [the electron has x-spin down] obtains. Neither proposal, however, tells us which state (or states) must obtain in order for 'the electron has x-spin up' to be indeterminate. What we are still lacking, in other words, is a theory of *indeterminate-makers*, which was the reason we brought in the hyperintensional approach in the first place.

Here is a way to address the problem. Say that states are *incompatible* if they cannot jointly obtain. Then,

HypeGap2. It is indeterminate whether p iff some state obtains that is incompatible with every truth-or-falsemaker for 'p'.

We know by MIN that HypeGap2-indeterminacy is metaphysical, as long as the semantics for the object language is precise. Also, HypeGap2 does not uphold bivalence, since 'p' can only be indeterminate when none of its truth-or-falsemakers obtains.

This proposal meets the aforementioned desideratum, in that it does not just specify necessary and sufficient indeterminacy conditions in terms of states, but it explains each instance of indeterminacy in terms of the obtaining of some particular state, the indeterminate-maker.

Let us now see how HypeGap2 deals with indeterminate composition. Recall that particle b from our example has momentum p. But the state [b has momentum p] is incompatible with [b is located at x'], hence with the fusion of [a is located at x] and [b is located at x'], for every x'. Therefore, some state obtains that is incompatible with every truth-or-falsemaker for 'a and b compose something'. HypeGap2 not only warrants the conclusion that it is metaphysically indeterminate whether a and b compose something, but also requires that we specify an indeterminate-maker, namely [b has momentum p]. HypeGap2 has therefore a clear explanatory advantage compared to the competition, hyperintensional or otherwise.

3.6 The Determinable-Based Account

3.6.1 Motivation

All theories of metaphysical indeterminacy considered in this section appeal to either truth-value gaps, a primitive notion of (in)determinacy, or Lewis-style modal realism. Wilson (2013) has articulated an alternative account that does not invoke any of those resources. Her account rests instead on a primitive distinction between determinable and determinate properties, which is best introduced by way of examples:

Having mass of 3.2 kg is a determinate of having mass.
Being magenta is a determinate of being red.
Being red is a determinate of being colored.

The relation of *determination*, which a determinate bears to each of its determinables, is typically taken to satisfy a number of constraints as a matter of necessity, which include the following:

i.   the determination relation defines a semilattice;[20]
ii. there are properties (red; triangular) that are determinables relative to some properties (magenta, vermillion; isosceles, equilateral), and determinates relative to others (colored; polygonal);
iii. there are atomic determinates – that is, determinates that are not determinables of any properties (PANTONE 19-1664 TPX; Euclidean equilateral triangle of side 1 m);
iv. if a has property P that is a determinate of Q, then a has Q;
v.   if a has properties P, Q, and P is a determinate of Q, then a has Q in virtue of having P;
vi. if a has determinable P, then a has some determinate of P;
vii. if a has determinable P, then a has at most one determinate of P.

Wilson argues that conditions v and vi don't hold by necessity, and that any counterexample to either of them constitutes an instance of metaphysical indeterminacy. More precisely, according to Wilson's determinable-based account,

DET. Metaphysical indeterminacy arises iff there is something a such that $\langle a$ is $Q \rangle$ obtains, and there is no unique P_i such that $\langle a$ is $P_i \rangle$ obtains

for Q a determinable, and $P_1, \ldots, P_n$ an exhaustive list of same-level determinates of Q.

---

[20] Namely, a strict partial order (irreflexive, asymmetric, transitive) such that any set of elements has a least upper bound. On the relation of determination, also see Calosi (2021).

Consequently, there are two ways for the world to display metaphysical indeterminacy. *Gappy* indeterminacy arises when something instantiates a determinable property Q but no same-level determinates of Q – in which case, condition vi will fail. A putative example of gappy indeterminacy is provided by the microscopic world. If photon a has a sharp value of momentum as a result of measurement at time t, orthodox quantum mechanics prescribes that no position value can be assigned to a at time t, on pain of inconsistency. According to Wilson, the photon at time t instantiates the position determinable, but none of its atomic determinates.

Metaphysical indeterminacy can also be *glutty*, namely when something instantiates a determinable property Q, as well as multiple same-level determinates of Q – in which case it is condition vii that fails. Wilson's favorite example is that of an "iridescent [hummingbird] feather whose color shifts from red to blue, depending on the angle of viewing" (2013, 367). She interprets this scenario in such a way that the feather has multiple determinate colors at all times, although an observer can perceive only one at any given time depending on the viewing angle. Thus, says Wilson, the feather instantiates both the color determinable and a number of atomic determinates of color, namely the particular shades of red, blue, and so forth. Since gappy and glutty indeterminacy are structurally similar, for the remainder of the discussion, I will focus on the former, unless noted otherwise. Note that, although an instance of DET-indeterminacy is either glutty or gappy, but not both, reality as a whole can in principle display both varieties.

According to Wilson, the determinable-based approach offers a reductive account of metaphysical indeterminacy, since it analyzes away the target phenomenon in terms of patters of instantiations of properties in the appropriate determination relations. Furthermore, the account is formulated against the background of a classical, bivalent, and compositional logic (Calosi & Wilson, 2019: 2601). In particular, suppose that the teapot has an indeterminate shade of red, in such a way that ⟨the teapot is R_i⟩ fails to obtain, for each atomic determinate R_i of red. It follows that ⟨the teapot is not R_i⟩ obtains, for each R_i – or else there will be a proposition such that neither it nor its negation obtains, against bivalence. It should be clear, then, that what Wilson calls 'gappy' indeterminacy has nothing to do with so-called truth-value gaps (and, likewise, that her 'glutty' indeterminacy involves no truth-value gluts).

3.6.2 From DET to DET$_{FUZZY}$

As it turns out, DET is unable to discriminate between possibilities that are quite clearly distinct. Consider a particle e with three possible values of the position determinable; call them *left*, *center*, and *right*. The two scenarios that any theory of indeterminacy should be able to distinguish are

Scenario 1: it is indeterminate whether e's position is left, center, or right.

Scenario 2: it is indeterminate whether e's position is left or center, whereas it is determinate that it is not right.

DET will model the two scenarios as follows:

Scenario 1 (DET): $\langle e$ has position$\rangle$ obtains; each of $\langle e$ is left$\rangle$, $\langle e$ is center$\rangle$, $\langle e$ is right$\rangle$ fails to obtain.

Scenario 2 (DET): $\langle e$ has position$\rangle$ obtains; each of $\langle e$ is left$\rangle$, $\langle e$ is center$\rangle$ fails to obtain; $\langle \neg (e$ is right$)\rangle$ obtains.

Wilson's view, in virtue of being bivalent, identifies $\langle p \rangle$'s not obtaining and $\langle \neg p \rangle$'s obtaining. Both scenarios will therefore reduce to

Scenario 1/2 (DET): $\langle e$ has position$\rangle$ obtains; each of $\langle e$ is left$\rangle$, $\langle e$ is center$\rangle$, $\langle e$ is right$\rangle$ fails to obtain.

Therefore, DET conflates both indeterminacy scenarios. The same kind of objection affects the glutty variety when the scenario are chosen as follows:

Scenario 1: it is indeterminate whether e's position is left, center, or right.

Scenario 3: it is indeterminate whether e's position is left or center, whereas it is determinate that it is right.

Since the argument is almost identical, the details are omitted.

One might reply by retreating to a variant of the determinable-determinate account involving fuzzy properties/propositions (Calosi & Wilson, 2021):

DET$_{\text{FUZZY}}$. Metaphysical indeterminacy arises iff there is something a such that $\langle a$ is $Q \rangle$ obtains, and there is some P_i such that $\langle a$ is P_i to degree $n \rangle$ obtains, for $0 < n < 1$

for Q a determinable, and P_1 *to degree 0, . . ., P_1 to degree 1, . . ., P_n to degree 0, . . ., P_n to degree 1* an exhaustive list of same-level determinates of Q.

Given DET$_{\text{FUZZY}}$, the three scenarios can be distinguished along the following lines:

Scenario 1 (DET$_{\text{FUZZY}}$): $\langle e$ has position$\rangle$ obtains; each of $\langle e$ is left to degree $1/3 \rangle$, $\langle e$ is center to degree $1/3 \rangle$, $\langle e$ is right to degree $1/3 \rangle$ obtains.

Scenario 2 (DET$_{\text{FUZZY}}$): $\langle e$ has position$\rangle$ obtains; each of $\langle e$ is left to degree $1/2\rangle$, $\langle e$ is center to degree $1/2\rangle$, $\langle e$ is right to degree $0\rangle$ obtains.

Scenario 3 (DET$_{\text{FUZZY}}$): $\langle e$ has position$\rangle$ obtains; each of $\langle e$ is left to degree $1/2\rangle$, $\langle e$ is center to degree $1/2\rangle$, $\langle e$ is right to degree $1\rangle$ obtains.

So far so good. Now, note that in stating DET$_{\text{FUZZY}}$ I have employed the schema

i) $\langle a$ is P to degree $n\rangle$ obtains

and not

ii) $\langle a$ is $P\rangle$ obtains to degree n.

For, necessarily, $\langle a$ is $P\rangle$ obtains to degree n iff 'a is P' is true to degree n. Therefore, ii is ruled out by the hypothesis of bivalence (cf. Calosi & Wilson, 2021: 3301n14). The ontology of DET$_{\text{FUZZY}}$ involves no degree-free determinate P, and so no degree-free proposition $\langle a$ is $P\rangle$.[21]

Nevertheless, degree-free propositions are straightforwardly defined into existence: just assume that, as a matter of necessity, ii holds iff i holds, for $0 \leq n \leq 1$. DET$_{\text{FUZZY}}$ will then be equivalent to

DET*$_{\text{FUZZY}}$. Metaphysical indeterminacy arises iff there is something a such that $\langle a$ is $Q\rangle$ obtains, and there is some P_i such that $\langle a$ is $P_i\rangle$ obtains to degree n, for $0 < n < 1$.

But insofar as DET*$_{\text{FUZZY}}$ captures indeterminacy in terms of indeterminately obtaining propositions, it is none other than a special case of IntGap (Section 3.3.1). Thus, although DET$_{\text{FUZZY}}$ manages to circumvent the aforementioned objection to gappy/glutty DET, there appears to be no metaphysically substantive difference between DET$_{\text{FUZZY}}$ and IntGap, with the exception that the latter is more general in that it does not appeal to the relation of determination.

3.6.3 Generality

A further worry targeting both DET and DET$_{\text{FUZZY}}$ is that they lack generality, in that a number of putative cases of metaphysical indeterminacy do not involve the relation of determination (cf. Barnes & Cameron, 2017).[22] Here are a few examples:

---

[21] Insofar as $\langle a$ is $P\rangle$ obtains iff a instantiates P, DET$_{\text{FUZZY}}$ had better not involve 'degrees of instantiation', pace Calosi and Wilson (2021).

[22] Lack of generality is a problem on the assumption that we can and should aim for a nondisjunctive characterization of metaphysical indeterminacy (Section 1.2).

Identity. Suppose that it is metaphysically indeterminate whether Kilimanjaro is k_1 or k_2. DET requires Kilimanjaro to have a determinable but none of the atomic determinates. Presumably, the relevant atomic determinates are the properties of being identical with k_1 and of being identical with k_2. However, it does not seem to be the case that identity properties are determinates of any determinable – not on the standard way of understanding the determinable-determinate relation, that is. Nor can the relevant determinable be identified with the property of being something. For if Kilimanjaro is something, it classically follows that Kilimanjaro is k, for some k, and so that having the determinable entails having some determinate, against the hypothesis.

Existence. Consider the organicist answer to the special composition question: things compose an object iff they constitute a life (van Inwagen, 1990: ch. 12). Do viruses exist? By the organicist's lights, there is no fact of the matter insofar as it is indeterminate whether a plurality S of mereological atoms arranged virus-wise compose a life. DET will then tell us that there is some thing having a determinable but none of the determinates. The thing cannot be the composite itself, however, for then it would exist, against the hypothesis (provided that something has a property only if it exists). Wilson (2017: 119n9) suggests that the determinable is had not by any individual object, but by the plurality S. If so, what is the determinable? According to Wilson, that would be the property of possibly composing an object, with determinables of composing and not composing an object. The answer is problematic in two ways. First, it follows that some things not composing an object possibly compose an object (by condition iv on the determinable-determinate distinction). But this is false on the standard assumption that composition is noncontingent. Second, possibility seems to be the wrong modality in this context insofar as we do not want to conflate indeterminacy with contingency. If the determinates are composing and not composing an object, the relevant determinable should rather be the property of not determinately not composing an object (i.e., the analog of possibly composing an object). However, this option is not open to Wilson, whose account does not feature a primitive (in)determinacy operator.

Open future. Say that it is indeterminate whether there will be a sea battle tomorrow. Once again, it is not clear how to make sense of such a claim in terms of patterns of determinable and determinate properties. As to the determinates: it cannot be the case that tomorrow's battle is such that it neither exists nor fails to exist; and the present cannot be such that it has neither the property of being such that there will be a sea battle nor the property of being such that there will not be a sea battle tomorrow. For both options are straightforwardly incompatible with the bivalence built into Wilson's account. Nor is it clear what determinable is suitable in this case, unless we stretch the notion of determinable to the point of becoming uninformative. The objection generalizes to all instances of indeterminacy involving a pair of mutually contradictory properties.

3.6.4 Sentential Operators

Finally, one might worry that Wilson's account flouts TEST (and so MIN). Suppose it is DET-indeterminate whether particle e is left or right. Since it is routine to regard 'it is indeterminate whether p or q' as short for 'it is indeterminate whether p and it is indeterminate whether q', it follows that

it is indeterminate whether the particle is left.

By TEST, we should conclude that

there is a proposition such that it is indeterminate whether it obtains.

On Wilson's account, however, no proposition can be such that it is indeterminate whether it obtains.

On the face of it, the worry is misplaced. Wilson will promptly reply that 'it is indeterminate whether e is left or right' should be paraphrased as 'e has the position determinable but neither the left position nor the right position determinate'. Thus, when it is indeterminate whether e is left or right, it is determinate that e is not left, and it is determinate that e is not right. TEST is satisfied, albeit vacuously.

Nevertheless, a twofold worry lingers. First, TEST is (vacuously) satisfied on the assumption that the standard paraphrase of 'it is indeterminate whether' is incorrect. That might well be the case, but then we need an error theory to explain away that, as well as similar common inferences. Second, the reply presupposes that 'it is indeterminate whether e is left or right' reduces to 'e has the position determinable but neither the left position nor the right position determinate'. Although that sounds plausible in the context of DET, it does not follow from it, since DET does not feature any (in)determinacy sentential operators, and so provides no guidance as to how such paraphrases ought to be carried out. In order to properly evaluate the account vis-à-vis MIN and TEST, we need general truth conditions for statements of the form 'it is indeterminate whether p' based on DET, for 'p' of arbitrary syntactical complexity. What such truth conditions would look like remains an open question.

4 Quantum Physics

4.1 Beyond Common Sense

There are at least three reasons why, among all putative manifestations of worldly indeterminacy, the quantum case enjoys a special status.

One is eminently metaphysical. Run-of-the-mill cases of worldly indeterminacy involve medium-sized dry goods, whether mountains or persons, which might lead one to believe that, if the world indeed displays indeterminacy, this can be resolved once we leave the ontology of common sense for the one of fundamental physics. For example, one may think that metaphysical indeterminacy is mereological in character (Section 2.1) and therefore that, while it is displayed by macroscopic objects, it is absent at the level of photons and quarks. As we will see, however, such a reassuring picture is challenged by quantum physics (cf. Lewis, 2016: ch. 4).

The second reason is methodological. The bulk of the literature on metaphysical indeterminacy, as well as the previous two sections of this Element, have focused on showing that the phenomenon is coherent. Coherence aside, the lingering doubt remains that indeterminacy concerning mountains and persons can be recast in semantic terms, and so that the evidence for metaphysical indeterminacy is far from compelling. As I will argue in Section 4.4, however, the prospects of casting quantum indeterminacy as a semantic, rather than worldly matter are slim.

The third reason why the quantum case stands out is epistemological. Why do we form the belief that Kilimanjaro is indeterminate? If our analysis is correct, because we neither accept nor reject 'Kilimanjaro is k', for some sharp mountain k, yet we take 'Kilimanjaro' (as well as 'k') to be referentially precise. Or perhaps because we neither accept nor reject 'j is part of Kilimanjaro', for some sharp rock j, yet we take 'Kilimanjaro' (as well as 'j') to be referentially precise. The evidence supporting Kilimanjaro's indeterminacy can then be factorized into an a priori and an a posteriori component. The former will comprise schematic linguistic intuitions such as

if both 'a' and 'b' are referentially determinate, and it is indeterminate whether $a = b$, then either a or b is indeterminate.

The a posteriori side is comprised of observational data about Kilimanjaro and surroundings.

When forming the belief that such and such quantum particles have indeterminate position, the situation is quite different. In this case, the a priori component involves general truths of pure mathematics, namely the general facts about the formalism in which the theory is couched. On the a posteriori side we find generalizations about the physical world, such as the *Schrödinger equation*, which specifies the dynamics of quantum systems, and the *Born rule*, which specifies the expectation values of quantum experiments; as well as empirical data supporting those generalizations, such as that the particles in the system at hand have been observed to have determinate values of momentum.

What sets apart the two cases is what we might call the *quality* of the available evidence. The evidence in support of quantum indeterminacy is of higher quality than the evidence for indeterminacy involving objects of common sense.

A priori evidence in the quantum case comprises the generalizations of mathematics, which have proven of enormous epistemic value toward understanding the world we live in. Moreover, belief in those generalizations is widely shared across cultures that may be very different otherwise. In the commonsense case, the relevant a priori evidence involves linguistic intuitions about whether a statement is (determinately) true or false, as well as intuitions about whether a term is referentially precise. Although such evidence plays a substantial role in our understanding of natural language, not only it lacks the abductive strength and cross-cultural stability of mathematical laws, but the very reliability of intuition, linguistic or otherwise, is constantly questioned.

When it comes to a posteriori evidence, although sense data about objects of common sense are easy to secure, they are of limited epistemic value, which explains why mature science has all but replaced them with precisely quantifiable data about theoretical objects, together with generalizations about those data.

On both counts, the available evidence is of higher quality in the case of fundamental physics than it is in the case of naïve physics. Therefore, any indeterminacy arising at the atomic and subatomic level is bound to have a special epistemic status. Because of that, it would be damning to a theory of indeterminacy if it were unable to account for indeterminacy of the quantum variety. As it turns out, among the theories discussed in Section 3, a number of them face precisely that problem. But first, let us introduce a few (very basic) notions from physics.

4.2 Hilbert Spaces

Quantum systems are modeled by way of *Hilbert spaces*, a generalization of Euclidean vector spaces (von Neumann, 1955).[23] The pure states of a system are identified with unitary vectors in Hilbert space. As per the orthodox interpretation of quantum mechanics, it will be assumed throughout that the formalism provides a complete representation of a quantum system. When systems are considered in isolation, a vector will then be a maximal state in the sense of Section 3.1 – that is, a world.

Two observations are in order. First, unlike a classical world, a quantum state cannot in general be decomposed into (does not supervene on) the states of the system's individual particles. In other words, quantum states are inherently holistic

---

[23] More precisely, a Hilbert space is a (finite or infinitely dimensional) inner product space that is complete with respect to the norm defined by the inner product.

(Teller, 1986). When such a decomposition is not possible, a system is said to be *entangled*. Second, unlike classical worlds, quantum states can in general be *superposed*. Whereas it makes classically no sense to say that the position of a particle is a 'mix' of different precise positions, things are otherwise at the microscopic level. Mathematically, quantum superposition corresponds to linear combination: if $\mathbf{u}$, $\mathbf{v}$ are states and α, β are complex numbers, $\alpha\mathbf{u} + \beta\mathbf{v}$ is also a state.

Quantum properties, aka observables – such as position, momentum, or spin in a particular spatial direction – are represented by a class of linear operators that go by the name of *Hermitian*. A vector $\mathbf{v}$ is said to be an *eigenstate* of Hermitian operator $\hat{O}$ if the application of $\hat{O}$ to $\mathbf{v}$ outputs $\lambda\mathbf{v}$, where λ is a real number called an *eigenvalue* of $\hat{O}$. Since the eigenstates of a Hermitian operator are pairwise orthogonal, a Hilbert space representing an observable with n eigenvalues is (at least) n-dimensional.

Let us consider an example (Figure 6). All particles that constitute matter (electrons, protons, neutrons, etc.) are spin-$\frac{1}{2}$ particles, spin being the quantum analog of angular momentum. Since spin-$\frac{1}{2}$ has two possible values, corresponding to the possible outcomes of being deflected either up or down on a measuring device, a spin-$\frac{1}{2}$ particle can be represented in a two-dimensional Hilbert space. For any spatial direction x in which spin can be measured, there exists a corresponding x-spin operator S_x with two eigenstates with eigenvalues 1 (up) and -1 (down), respectively. We will refer to these eigenstates as $[\uparrow_x]$ and $[\downarrow_x]$. Since states can be superposed, our Hilbert space also contains superpositions of $[\uparrow_x]$ and $[\downarrow_x]$, namely the eigenstates of the y-spin operator S_y with

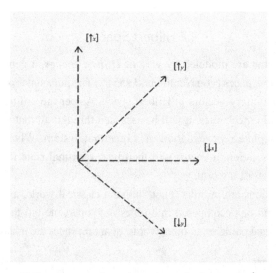

Figure 6 Eigenstates of x-spin and y-spin for a spin-$\frac{1}{2}$ particle

eigenvalues 1 (up) and −1 (down), respectively. We will refer to these eigenstates as [↑$_y$] and [↓$_y$].

How do physical observables of a system S relate to their mathematical counterparts, the Hermitian operators? The orthodox answer is provided by the following criterion, known as the *eigenstate-eigenvalue link* (Gilton, 2016):

EEL. 'S has property O with value λ' is true iff the state vector of S is in an eigenstate of the associated Hermitian operator $\hat{O}$ with eigenvalue λ.

Accordingly, the system from the example has the property of being x-spin up just when the state vector is [↑$_x$].

A distinctive feature of classical mechanics is *value definiteness*, the fact that each observable of a system has a determinate value at all times. For instance, classical particles always have both position and momentum – which explains why we can ascribe them trajectories in space-time. Quantum systems, on the other hand, lack value definiteness. By EEL, we can only ascribe a determinate value of some property to a system when the state vector is an eigenstate of the relevant operator. An electron that is observed to have a determinate value of x-spin finds itself in some eigenstate of S_x, and so in no eigenstate of S_y; therefore, it has no determinate value of y-spin (and vice versa).

Far from being exceptions, such scenarios are in fact the norm. For every quantum property O there is some complementary property O' such that O and O' cannot both have determinate values for a given system at the same time (cf. Section 3.5.1).

The lack of value definiteness has been interpreted with varying degrees of confidence as evidence of quantum metaphysical indeterminacy (Darby, 2010; Skow, 2010; Bokulich, 2014; Wolff, 2015; Lewis, 2016; Barrett, 2019. Calosi & Wilson, 2019; Torza, 2020a, 2021; Calosi & Mariani, 2021; Calosi & Wilson, 2021; Darby & Pickup, 2021; Fletcher and Taylor, 2021a; Schroeren, 2021). When electron e has value up of x-spin, but no value of y-spin, it is indeed tempting to read the situation in such a way that

i)   it is determinate that e has x-spin up;
ii) it is indeterminate whether e has y-spin up or y-spin down.

Whether and how we can do justice to such a reading is going to depend on the underlying theory of metaphysical indeterminacy.

Before we delve into such questions, two caveats are in order. First, it is important to stress what quantum metaphysical indeterminacy is not: it is not the thesis that it can be indeterminate what state a system is in. That is always determinate, because it is always determinate which vector in Hilbert space represents the obtaining state of a given system. What quantum indeterminacy involves is that the value of some observable can be indeterminate. In other words, the thesis under scrutiny is that it can be indeterminate whether a system S instantiates some property O with value λ.

Second, we will be restricting our attention to orthodox quantum mechanics, as defined by the conjunction of the following conditions (Wallace, 2019):

a. the Schrödinger equation, which describes the time evolution of the state of a quantum system, except when measurement occurs;
b. the collapse postulate, according to which measuring an observable O will make the state jump to one of the eigenstates of the associated operator $\hat{O}$ according to the probabilities specified by the Born rule;
c. EEL.

Insofar as we will be taking metaphysics lessons from it, orthodox quantum mechanics will need to be interpreted realistically. Although a realist attitude is not commonly associated with the orthodoxy, it is by no means ruled out either (cf. Bokulich, 2014: 460n14; Schroeren, 2021).[24] In what follows it will be assumed that realism about orthodox quantum mechanics involves a condition known as the *reality criterion* (Einstein, Podolsky & Rosen, 1935: 777):

If the probability that p is 1, then there is an element of reality that makes it so that p.

Although the reality criterion is by no means unavoidable (Glick & Boge, 2021), it is arguably analytic given a realist attitude toward quantum theory (Maudlin, 2014).

4.3 Modeling Quantum Metaphysical Indeterminacy

4.3.1 Quantum Truthmaker Semantics

In order to evaluate whether orthodox quantum mechanics provides evidence of metaphysical indeterminacy, we need to be able to assign semantic values to empirical statements – that is, statements ascribing empirical properties to quantum systems. (A property is empirical if there are experimental sufficient conditions for its ascription.) Following the methodology of Section 3.5, the ensuing discussion will be phrased in terms of fine-grained content, although similar conclusions can be drawn by employing a coarse-grained notion of content.

---

[24] The issue of quantum indeterminacy can and has been studied beyond the orthodoxy: in the many-world interpretation (Calosi & Wilson, 2022), GRW (Mariani, 2022b), the modal interpretations (Calosi, 2022), and relational quantum mechanics (Calosi & Mariani, 2020).

The go-to method to formulate a semantics for empirical statements is provided by quantum logic (Birkhoff & von Neumann, 1936). The quantum-logical approach can be restated in truthmaker-theoretic guise as follows:

i. state **v** is a truthmaker for the atomic empirical statement '*S* has property *O* with value λ' iff **v** is an eigenstate of $\hat{O}$ with eigenvalue λ.

ii. state **v** is a truthmaker for the conjunctive empirical statement '*q* $\wedge$ *r*', iff **v** is a truthmaker for both '*q*' and '*r*'.

iii. state **v** is a truthmaker for the negated empirical statement '$\neg q$' iff **v** is orthogonal to every truthmaker for '*q*'.

The disjunction '*q* $\vee$ *r*' is defined as '$\neg(\neg q \wedge \neg r)$'. It follows that **v** is a truthmaker for '*q* $\vee$ *r*' iff it is a superposition (linear combination) of a truthmaker for '*q*' and a truthmaker for '*r*'.

Clause i guarantees that EEL is satisfied. Clause ii states that quantum conjunction operates just like its classical counterpart. Clause iii is where quantum truthmaker semantics departs most decisively from classical logic. Classically, the truthmakers for '$\neg q$' are all and only states that are incompatible with a truthmaker for '*q*'. For example, the state [the mug is magenta] is a classical truthmaker for 'the mug is not blue' because it cannot co-obtain with any truthmaker for 'the mug is blue'. In the quantum case, every truthmaker for '$\neg q$' is incompatible with a truthmaker for '*q*', but not the other way around. Quantum negation is therefore stronger than its classical counterpart. For example, the state $[\uparrow_y]$ is incompatible with $[\uparrow_x]$, which is a truthmaker for '*e* has *x*-spin up', yet $[\uparrow_y]$ is not a truthmaker for '*e* does not have *x*-spin up'. The reason for such revisionism about negation lies in Born's rule, the recipe for assigning probabilistic values to experimental statements. Born's rule entails, for any empirical statement '*p*', that

A. if the probability that *p* if $\mathbf{v_a}$ obtains is 1, the probability that *p* if $\mathbf{v_b}$ obtains is 1, and **v** is a linear combination of $\mathbf{v_a}$ and $\mathbf{v_b}$, then the probability that *p* if **v** obtains is also 1 (Dalla Chiara & Giuntini, 2002).

Now, assume that the following thesis, linking experimental certainty to the truth of experimental statements, holds as a matter of necessity:

B. **v** is a truthmaker for '*p*' iff the probability that *p* if **v** obtains is 1.

The left-to-right direction of B is self-evident, as well as following from truthmaker necessitarianism (Section 3.1), whereas its converse corresponds to the reality criterion.[25] It is a straightforward consequence of A and B that

---

[25] This much should be uncontentious: there is an element of reality that makes it so that *p* iff there is an element of reality that makes '*p*' true iff there is a truthmaker for '*p*'. Given the realist assumption that quantum states are the truthmakers for quantum statements: there is a truthmaker

C. if $\mathbf{v}_a$ is a truthmaker for 'p', $\mathbf{v}_b$ is a truthmaker for 'p', and $\mathbf{v}$ is a linear combination of $\mathbf{v}_a$ and $\mathbf{v}_b$, then $\mathbf{v}$ is a truthmaker for 'p'.

In other words, C guarantees that truthmaking is closed under linear combination. As it turns out, this closure condition suffices to rule out the classical interpretation of negation for the experimental statements of quantum mechanics.

In order to see that, suppose that the truthmakers for 'e does not have x-spin up' are the states incompatible with $[\uparrow_x]$, that is to say, those states that differ from $[\uparrow_x]$ by more than just a scalar multiple. In particular, both $[\uparrow_y]$ and $[\downarrow_y]$ will be truthmakers for 'e does not have x-spin up'. Since $[\uparrow_x]$ is a linear combination of $[\uparrow_y]$ and $[\downarrow_y]$, it follows by C that $[\uparrow_x]$ is a truthmaker for 'e does not have x-spin up'. As we know from clause i, however, $[\uparrow_x]$ is also a truthmaker for 'e has x-spin up'. So, by clause ii, $[\uparrow_x]$ is a truthmaker for 'e does and does not have x-spin up'. Contradiction. (A similar argument shows that disjunction cannot be interpreted classically either.)

The moral is that quantum truthmaker semantics should be chosen over the classical alternative, once Born's rule and the reality criterion are factored in. Let us move ahead.

A *Hilbert model* $H_{\mathcal{L}}$ for an empirical language $\mathcal{L}$ is a Hilbert space that has a designated state (the obtaining state[26]), and specifies truthmaking conditions for all statements of $\mathcal{L}$ as per clauses i–iii. For any statement 'p' of $\mathcal{L}$, we say that:

- 'p' is *true* in $H_{\mathcal{L}}$ if the obtaining state is a truthmaker for 'p';
- 'p' is *logically true* if it is true in every Hilbert model;
- 'p' is a *logical consequence* of a set of $\mathcal{L}$-statements Δ if 'p' is true in every Hilbert model where each member of Δ is true;
- 'p' and 'q' are *logically equivalent* if each is a logical consequence of the other.

Consider now a model $H_{\mathcal{L}}$ for the single-electron system from Section 4.2. When the obtaining state is $[\uparrow_x]$, and given the routine convention of identifying the falsity of a statement with the truth of its negation, the model yields the following truth value assignments:

E1. 'e has x-spin up' is true;

E2. 'e does not have x-spin up' is false;

---

for 'p' iff some state is a truthmaker for 'p'. By EEL plus the fact that the probability that p if $\mathbf{v}$ obtains is 1: some state is the truthmaker for 'p' iff $\mathbf{v}$ is a truthmaker for 'p'. Hence, the reality criterion and the right-to-left direction of B are equivalent.

[26] Which state obtains is a function of time – a detail that is left out in order to streamline the exposition.

E3. '*e* has *x*-spin down' is false;

E4. '*e* has *y*-spin up' is neither true nor false;

E5. '*e* has either *y*-spin up or *y*-spin down' is true;

E6. '*e* has either *x*-spin up or *x*-spin down' is true.

The least obvious assignments are the last three. E4 is the case because $[\uparrow_x]$ is not an eigenstate of the *y*-spin operator S_y. E5 is the case because the model is spanned by the eigenstates of S_y, and so $[\uparrow_x]$ is a linear combination of a truthmaker for '*e* has *y*-spin up' and a truthmaker for '*e* has *y*-spin down' (namely $[\uparrow_x] = \frac{1}{\sqrt{2}}([\uparrow_y] + [\downarrow_y])$). In fact, since the same line of thought applies to every model of the given language, '*e* has either *y*-spin up or *y*-spin down' is a logical truth. The reasoning carries over to E6 insofar as the model is spanned by the eigenstates of S_x.

It is also worth noting that '*e* does not have *x*-spin up' and '*e* has *x*-spin down' are logically equivalent, since in every model H_ϱ they are made true by the same state, namely $[\downarrow_x]$.

Here are some of the distinguishing logical properties of an experimental language interpreted in terms of quantum truthmaker semantics. First of all, the logic that emerges is nonclassical, since it does not validate the distribution laws

$$p \wedge (q \vee r) \text{ iff } (p \wedge q) \vee (p \wedge r)$$
$$p \vee (q \wedge r) \text{ iff } (p \vee q) \wedge (p \vee r).$$

Nevertheless, a number of classical equivalences are preserved, such as the law of double negation:

$$p \text{ iff } \neg\neg p.$$

The class of quantum-logical truths includes the law of excluded middle, as well as the law of noncontradiction:

$$p \vee \neg p$$

$$\neg(p \wedge \neg p).$$

Quantum truthmaker semantics is not bivalent, as exemplified by E4. It is not truth-functional either. For instance, consider once again the model H_ϱ for a single electron in the *x*-spin up state, and let '*p*' be '*e* has *y*-spin up', which is neither true nor false in H_ϱ. Trivially, '$p \vee \neg p$' is true in H_ϱ. On the other hand, '$p \vee p$' is logically equivalent to '*p*', and so neither true nor false in H_ϱ. Hence, '$p \vee \neg p$' and '$p \vee p$' have distinct truth values, despite the fact that the latter is obtained from the former by substituting the sentence '$\neg p$' for one with the same truth value, namely '*p*'.

Now that the semantic and logical machinery has been sketched, the crucial question can finally be addressed: does metaphysical indeterminacy arise in quantum mechanics? According to the hyperintensional gappy theories of Section 3.5, the answer is a straightforward yes. Consider HypeGap2, the thesis that it is metaphysically indeterminate whether p just in case some state obtains that is incompatible with every truth-or-falsemaker for 'p'. In the above model $H_{\mathcal{Q}}$, the set of truth-or-falsemakers for 'e has y-spin up' is $T = \{[\uparrow_y], [\downarrow_y]\}$. Since $[\uparrow_x]$ obtains and is incompatible with every member of T, it is HypeGap2-indeterminate whether e has y-spin up. The same conclusion can be drawn from HypeGap1, the thesis that it is metaphysically indeterminate whether p just in case no truth-or-falsemaker for 'p' obtains.[27]

What about hyperintensional bivalent theories? According to Hype2, it is metaphysically indeterminate whether p just in case some truth-or-falsemaker for 'p' indeterminately obtains, and none determinately obtains. As already observed, however, in a Hilbert model, there is no such thing as indeterminately obtaining states. The same remarks apply to Hype1.

4.3.2 'Deep' Indeterminacy

Advocates of Hype1/2 will presumably react by searching for a suitable revision of quantum truthmaker semantics that makes room for indeterminacy while upholding bivalence. Given fairly sensible assumptions, however, hyperintensional bivalent theories of metaphysical indeterminacy are provably unable to account for indeterminacy of the quantum variety, no matter which truthmaker semantics they are paired with.

Suppose that metaphysical indeterminacy arises in our single-electron system in such a way that:

1. It is determinate that e has x-spin up.
2. It is indeterminate whether e has y-spin up or y-spin down.

It immediately follows from 2 that

3. It is indeterminate whether e has y-spin up.

Let us now assume Hype1, the thesis that it is metaphysically indeterminate whether p iff some truthmaker for 'p' indeterminately obtains, and none determinately obtains. It follows from 3 and Hype1 that

---

[27] *Mutatis mutandis* the same conclusion can be drawn in the coarse-grained counterpart of HypeGap1/2, namely IntGap, as well as in DET_{FUZZY} (for recall that DET_{FUZZY} is equivalent with DET^*_{FUZZY}, which is subsumed by IntGap).

4. There is a truthmaker for 'e has y-spin up' such that it is indeterminate whether it obtains.

Because the system's only truthmaker for 'e has y-spin up' is $[\uparrow_y]$, 4 entails:

5. It is indeterminate whether $[\uparrow_y]$ obtains.

Because the system's only truthmaker for 'e has x-spin up' is $[\uparrow_x]$, 1 entails:

6. It is determinate that $[\uparrow_x]$ obtains.

By the determinacy of distinctness,

7. It is determinate that $[\uparrow_x] \neq [\uparrow_y]$.

Provided that 'determinate that' and 'indeterminate whether' are analogous to 'necessary that' and 'contingent whether', lines 5, 6 and 7 jointly entail that

8. It is indeterminate whether ($[\uparrow_x]$ obtains and $[\uparrow_y]$ obtains and $[\uparrow_x] \neq [\uparrow_y]$)

hence

9. It is not determinate that not ($[\uparrow_x]$ obtains and $[\uparrow_y]$ obtains and $[\uparrow_x] \neq [\uparrow_y]$).

Quantum states being maximal, they are mutually exclusive:

10. It is determinate that, if $\mathbf{v}$ obtains and $\mathbf{v'}$ obtains, then $\mathbf{v} = \mathbf{v'}$

hence,

11. It is determinate that (if $[\uparrow_x]$ obtains and $[\uparrow_y]$ obtains, then $[\uparrow_x] = [\uparrow_y]$).

Lines 9 and 11 are truth-functionally incompatible, which concludes the *reductio* of Hype1. The same kind of proof provides a *reductio* of Hype2 and, with a few modifications, of intensional bivalent characterizations of metaphysical indeterminacy (IntConc1/2, IntErsatz).

A few observations are in order. The crux of the argument is the inference from line 3 to line 4. In order to preserve bivalence in the object language, bivalent theories characterize indeterminacy by appealing to (in)determinacy operators in the metalanguage, where it is asserted that some state indeterminately obtains. As already observed, however, quantum mechanics nowhere entails or even suggests that a state may indeterminately obtain. Quantum indeterminacy is not indeterminacy as to whether any particular state obtains. As the argument shows, assuming otherwise leads to inconsistency.

Line 7 can be resisted if the determinacy of distinctness is denied. For example, one may follow Akiba and reject the B schema $\phi \rightarrow \mathbf{D}\neg\mathbf{D}\neg\phi$, which licenses the inference from the determinacy of identity to the determinacy of distinctness

(Section 2.4.5). This route, although open to the advocate of bivalent theories, is hardly viable, as the quantum formalism provides no reason to believe that distinct quantum states might be identical (in the relevant sense of 'might'). Moreover, advocates of bivalent theories, whether intensional (Barnes & Williams, 2011: 111) or hyperintensional (Barnes, 2010: 603), have been explicit in their intention to decouple the general question of metaphysical indeterminacy from the particular questions of indeterminate identity and distinctness.

Line 8 relies on the assumption that the inference

$$\nabla p, \mathbf{D}q \vdash \nabla(p \wedge q).$$

is valid in the metatheory, which is guaranteed as long as the (in)determinacy operators behave like standard modal operators, a view that has been defended across the spectrum of bivalent theories, and specifically by Barnes (2010: 625n58), advocate of Hype1, who takes the logic of (in)determinacy to be S5.

Line 10 is justified on the assumption that (i) quantum states are maximal, and that, (ii) determinately, distinct maximal states do not co-obtain.[28] Condition i captures the idea that a Hilbert space provides a complete description of a quantum system. One may then resist the argument by insisting that orthodox quantum mechanics is descriptively incomplete, and so that there is more to a physical system than can be packed in a Hilbert space. If that is the case, there ought to be some *hidden-variable theory*, that is to say, a reformulation of quantum mechanics that completes the picture by introducing extra physical structure. As soon as i is rejected, $[\uparrow_x]$ and $[\uparrow_y]$ may be able to co-obtain.

The quest for hidden-variable theories is a classical topic in the history of quantum physics, which dates back to Einstein, Podolsky, and Rosen (1935). As a number of negative results would eventually show, however, any hidden-variable theory inevitably leads to the violation of one or more crucial physical conditions (Bell, 1966; Kochen & Specker, 1967). Be that as it may, since the issue that presently concerns us is how to model indeterminacy arising within orthodox quantum mechanics, appealing to hidden-variables is dialectically beside the point.

One final observation. Although arguments to the effect that bivalent theories of metaphysical indeterminacy fail to account for the quantum case are not new (Darby, 2010; Skow, 2010; Corti, 2021), they have been aimed exclusively at precisificational theories of indeterminacy, especially IntErsatz. Because of

---

[28] Condition ii should not be conflated with the modal thesis that distinct quantum states are incompatible – that is, that, necessarily, they do not co-obtain.

that, the conclusion that has been drawn is that quantum indeterminacy is too 'deep' to be resolved in terms of (ontic) precisifications.

That conclusion, however, misdiagnoses the ailment. The problem with bivalent precisificational theories is not that they are precisificational but that they uphold bivalence by glossing indeterminacy in terms of indeterminately obtaining states. This conclusion is backed by two facts. One is that the aforementioned *reductio* is carried out without presupposing any precisificational machinery. The other is that Wilson's determinable-based account (DET), which upholds bivalence, avoids the *reductio* precisely because it does not postulate indeterminately obtaining states. Recall that DET analyzes away metaphysical indeterminacy by way of appropriate patterns of (determinately) obtaining and (determinately) non-obtaining states of affairs. As a consequence, the inference from line 3 to line 4 is bound to fail. Relatedly, the inference to line 8 is also unwarranted since, according to DET, 'determinate that' and 'indeterminate whether' do not behave like standard modal operators. (However, see (Fletcher & Taylor, 2021a: 11196) for an argument to the effect that DET is incompatible with EEL.)

4.4 Against 'Against Quantum Indeterminacy'

The foregoing discussion started from the observation that the failure of value definiteness in quantum physics provides prima facie evidence for metaphysical indeterminacy. By suitably pairing a truthmaker semantics and a theory of metaphysical indeterminacy, it was shown how that hypothesis could be substantiated – and how it could not.

But what if we were on the wrong track all along, and quantum systems are best understood as not involving any metaphysical indeterminacy? There are two readings of that worry. One could argue that, while there may be some evidence for metaphysical indeterminacy, it is trumped by countervailing considerations. Alternatively, it could be argued that the evidence, if at all conclusive, is compatible with the existence of representational, rather than metaphysical indeterminacy.

Here is a way to make the worry's first reading precise. Quantum indeterminacy is indeterminacy as to which values of an observable is instantiated. According to the orthodox interpretation of quantum mechanics, the value of an observable is grounded in which state obtains, which, as already observed, is never indeterminate. So, goes the objection, the indeterminacy is metaphysically derivative, in that it only affects nonfundamental facts about the observables, rather than fundamental facts about the obtaining of states. This picture therefore supports an eliminativist stance toward quantum indeterminacy (Glick, 2017).

However, the fact that some phenomenon X is derivative by no means warrants a form of eliminativism about X. Tables and chairs are indisputably derivative, namely by being grounded in their subatomic components, yet we hardly doubt their existence (pace the nihilists, mereological and otherwise). In fact, the very existence of some sort of grounding relation linking the fundamental and the derivative require the existence of both *relata*. Considerations of metaphysical priority therefore presuppose, rather than undermine, that the derivative exists.

The objector could bolster up the argument with the extra thesis, defended in Barnes (2014), that if there is no fundamental metaphysical indeterminacy, there is no metaphysical indeterminacy, period. Such a move would rule out the possibility of derivative quantum indeterminacy, provided that the obtaining and non-obtaining of states is perfectly determinate.

However, Barnes's defense of the thesis is framed within her own bivalent theory of indeterminacy, which, as we saw, is a poor choice for modeling the quantum case. Moreover, recall that, according to Barnes (2010), for it to be metaphysically indeterminate whether p, there must be a truthmaker for 'p' that indeterminately obtains. When 'p' is a sentence expressing the instantiation of a quantum property, such as 'e is x-spin up', its truthmaker $[\uparrow_x]$ will then have to indeterminately obtain, against Glick's (and our) observation that quantum states either determinately obtain, or determinately fail to obtain.

Finally, it is worth mentioning, contra Barnes, that there is a number of ways to make sense of merely derivative metaphysical indeterminacy, both in general and in the specific case of quantum physics (Mariani, 2021, 2022a; Torza, 2022).

Moving on to the second reading of this worry, one might attempt to deflate the indeterminacy thesis by turning it into a merely representational matter. This reading mirrors the strategy that can be adopted in the macroscopic case: just like indeterminacy involving Kilimanjaro could be construed as arising from the semantics of statements about Kilimanjaro, likewise indeterminacy involving an electron's spin could be construed as arising from the semantics of statements about an electron's spin. The strategy, if successful, would significantly weaken the evidence for the thesis that quantum indeterminacy originates in the world rather than in our representation.

In order to assess the strategy, we need a way to assign semantic values to empirical statements in a way that makes room for semantic indeterminacy. That can be done by drawing on Finean supervaluations. If H is a Hilbert space associated with system S, and $\mathcal{L}$ is a language about S, a valuation V for $\mathcal{L}$ satisfies (at least) the following conditions:

i. the set of truthmakers for the atomic empirical statement 'S has property O with value λ' includes each eigenstate of $\hat{O}$ with eigenvalue λ.

ii. the set of truthmakers for the conjunctive empirical statement '$q \wedge r$' is the intersection of the set of truthmakers for 'q' and the set of truthmakers for 'r'.

iii. the set of truthmakers for the negated empirical statement '$\neg q$' is the complement in H of the set of truthmakers for 'q'.

iv. if the probability that q given $\mathbf{v} \geq$ the probability of q given $\mathbf{v}$' then, if $\mathbf{v}$' is a truthmaker for 'q', so is $\mathbf{v}$.

The disjunction '$q \vee r$' is defined as '$\neg(\neg q \wedge \neg r)$'. It follows that the set of truthmakers for '$q \vee r$' is the union of the set of truthmakers for 'q' and the set of truthmakers for 'r'.

Clause i tells us that being an eigenstate of $\hat{O}$ with eigenvalue λ is a sufficient, though not necessary condition for 'S has property O with value λ' to be true. Consequently, the present semantics does not validate EEL.[29] Conditions ii and iii guarantee that valuations are logically classical. Condition iv encodes the penumbral connections that are to be expected in the quantum realm: as the probability of q increases as a function of the system's state, the truth value of 'q' can only change from False to True.

A *Fine-Hilbert model* $F_{\mathcal{L}}$ for an empirical language $\mathcal{L}$ is a Hilbert space with a designated state (the obtaining state), and a set of valuations $V_{i \in I}$ for the statements of $\mathcal{L}$ satisfying conditions i–iv. For any statement 'p' of $\mathcal{L}$, we say that:

- 'p' is *true* in $F_{\mathcal{L}}$ if, on every valuation $V_{i \in I}$, the set of truthmakers for 'p' includes the obtaining state; 'p' is *false* in $F_{\mathcal{L}}$ if, on every valuation $V_{i \in I}$, the set of truthmakers for '$\neg p$' includes the obtaining state; otherwise, 'p' is *indeterminate* in $F_{\mathcal{L}}$;
- 'p' is *logically true* if it is true in every Fine-Hilbert model;
- 'p' is a *logical consequence* of a set of $\mathcal{L}$-statements Δ if 'p' is true in every Fine-Hilbert model where each member of Δ is true;
- 'p' and 'q' are *logically equivalent* if each is a logical consequence of the other.

Can quantum indeterminacy be construed as a semantic phenomenon by appealing to Fine-Hilbert models? The trouble with the semantics just sketched is that it violates condition C from Section 4.3.1. Indeed, if 'p' is indeterminate in a Fine-Hilbert model, there is a valuation V such that either the set of truthmakers for 'p' or the set of truthmakers for '$\neg p$' fails to be closed under linear combination.

---

[29] Note that parting with EEL need not mean that the orthodoxy is lost (cf. Wallace, 2019).

In order to see that, consider a Fine-Hilbert model $F_{\mathcal{Q}}$ for an empirical language about a single-electron system. If, say, 'e has x-spin up' is indeterminate, there is an assignment V that makes it false. By clause iii, $[\uparrow_y]$ is either a truthmaker or a falsemaker for 'e has x-spin up' in V. If the former, $[\downarrow_y]$ is also a truthmaker for 'e has x-spin up' in V, by clause iv. Therefore, the truthmakers for 'e has x-spin up' in V span H. Because 'e has x-spin up' is false in V, not all states are truthmakers for it in V. So the truthmakers for 'e has x-spin up' in V are not closed under linear combination. If, on the other hand, $[\uparrow_y]$ is a falsemaker for 'e has x-spin up' in V, so is $[\downarrow_y]$, by iv. It follows that the falsemakers for 'e has x-spin up' in V span H. Since, by clause i, 'e has x-spin up' has truthmakers in V, not all states are falsemakers for it in V. So, the falsemakers for 'e has x-spin up' in V are not closed under linear combination. QED.

Because the closure condition was inferred from the conjunction of A and B, either of these will break down in Fine-Hilbert semantics. On closer inspection, what fails is B's left-to-right direction, the thesis that

if **v** is a truthmaker for 'p', the probability that p if **v** obtains is 1.

For example, when 'e has x-spin up' is indeterminate in virtue of e's having y-spin up, there will be a valuation V on which $[\uparrow_y]$ is a truthmaker for 'e has x-spin up', although the probability that e is observed to have x-spin up upon measurement given $[\uparrow_y]$ is less than 1. Insofar as B's left-to-right direction is false on some valuation, it is untrue *simpliciter*.

Can the advocate of the semanticist solution bite the bullet and drop B's left-to-right direction? Since that conditional is a fairly uncontroversial assumption about the truth-probability link, any attempt at capturing quantum indeterminacy in semantic terms will have to provide a revisionary, yet compelling story as to how truth and probability fit together.

5 Concluding Remarks

We have addressed two key questions concerning indeterminacy in the world: whether it can arise, and whether it in fact arises.

Contrary to the view that used to be mainstream in the twentieth century, metaphysical indeterminacy is possible insofar as it can be made sense of and coherently theorized about, whether in terms of indeterminate objects (Section 2), or indeterminate states of affairs (Section 3). There also exists evidence that it is actual insofar as, on the most promising characterizations of metaphysical indeterminacy (HypeGap1/2), it follows from the orthodox interpretation of quantum mechanics (Section 4).

One potential worry is that alleged instances of metaphysical indeterminacy could be redescribed as instances of semantic indeterminacy, so the evidence is far from conclusive. For example, metaphysical indeterminacy as to whether Kilimanjaro is so and so could in principle be eliminated in favor of semantic indeterminacy about the truth of 'Kilimanjaro is so and so', provided that 'Kilimanjaro' is referentially imprecise. As argued in Section 4.4, however, such deflationary strategies are not easily available in the quantum case.

References

Akiba, K. (2000). Vagueness as a modality. *Philosophical Quarterly*, 50(200), 359–370.

Akiba, K. (2004). Vagueness in the world. *Noûs*, 38(3), 407–429.

Akiba, K. (2014a). A defense of indeterminate distinctness. *Synthese*, 191(15), 3557–3573.

Akiba, K. (2014b) Introduction. In K. Akiba & A. Abasnezhad, eds., *Vague Objects and Vague Identity: New Essays on Ontic Vagueness*. Dordrecht: Springer 1–21.

Akiba, K. (2017). A unification of two approaches to vagueness: The Boolean many-valued approach and the modal-precisificational approach. *Journal of Philosophical Logic*, 46(4), 419–441.

Akiba, K. (2022). The Boolean many-valued solution to the sorites paradox. *Synthese*, 200(2), 1–25.

Aristotle (1963). *Aristotle in Twenty-Three Volumes*. Loeb Classical Library. Cambridge, MA: Harvard University Press.

Armstrong, D. M. (2004). *Truth and Truthmakers*. Cambridge: Cambridge University Press.

Barker, S. (2014). Semantic paradox and alethic undecidability. *Analysis*, 74(2), 201–209.

Barnes, E. (2009). Indeterminacy, identity and counterparts: Evans reconsidered. *Synthese*, 168(1), 81–96.

Barnes, E. (2010). Ontic vagueness: A guide for the perplexed. *Noûs*, 44(4), 601–627.

Barnes, E. (2013). Metaphysically indeterminate existence. *Philosophical Studies*, 166(3), 495–510.

Barnes, E. (2014). Fundamental indeterminacy. *Analytic Philosophy*, 55(4), 339–362.

Barnes, E. & Cameron, R. (2008). The open future: Bivalence, determinism and ontology. *Philosophical Studies*, 146(2), 291–309.

Barnes, E. & Cameron, R. (2017). Are there indeterminate states of affairs? No. In E. Barnes, ed., *Current Controversies in Metaphysics*. London: Routledge, pp. 120–131.

Barnes, E. & Williams, J. R. G. (2009). Vague parts and vague identity. *Pacific Philosophical Quarterly*, 90(2), 176–187.

Barnes, E. & Williams, J. R. G. (2011). A theory of metaphysical indeterminacy. In K. Bennett, K. & D. W. Zimmerman, eds., *Oxford Studies in Metaphysics*, vol. 6. Oxford: Oxford University Press, pp. 103–148.

Barrett, J. A. (2019). The Conceptual Foundations of Quantum Mechanics. Oxford, UK: Oxford University Press.

Bell, J. S. (1966). On the problem of hidden variables in quantum mechanics. *Reviews of Modern Physics*, 38, 447–452.

Bernstein, S. (2016). Causal and moral indeterminacy. *Ratio*, 29(4), 434–447.

Birkhoff, G. & von Neumann, J. (1936). The logic of quantum mechanics. *Annals of Mathematics*, 823–843 Vol. 37, No. 4

Bokulich, A. (2014). Metaphysical indeterminacy, properties, and quantum theory. *Res Philosophica*, 91(3), 449–475.

Boolos, G. (1984). To be is to be a value of a variable (or to be some values of some variables). *Journal of Philosophy*, 81(8), 430–449.

Bradley, S. (2016). Vague chance? *Ergo*, 3(20), 524–538.

Burgess, J. A. (1990). Vague objects and indefinite identity. *Philosophical Studies*, 59(3), 263–287.

Caie, M. (2014). Metasemantics and metaphysical indeterminacy. In A. Burgess & B. Sherman, eds., *Metasemantics: New Essays on the Foundations of Meaning*. Oxford: Oxford University Press, pp. 55–96.

Calosi, C. (2021). Gappy, glutty, glappy. *Synthese*, 199(3–4), 11305–11321.

Calosi, C. (2022). Quantum modal indeterminacy. *Studies in History and Philosophy of Science Part A*, 95, 177–184.

Calosi, C. & Mariani, C. (2020). Quantum relational indeterminacy. *Studies in History and Philosophy of Science Part B: Studies in History and Philosophy of Modern Physics*, 71, 158–169.

Calosi, C. & Mariani, C. (2021). Quantum indeterminacy. *Philosophy Compass*, 16(4), e12731.

Calosi, C. & Wilson, J. M. (2019). Quantum metaphysical indeterminacy. *Philosophical Studies*, 176(10), 2599–2627.

Calosi, C. & Wilson, J. M. (2021). Quantum indeterminacy and the double-slit experiment. *Philosophical Studies*, 178(10), 3291–3317.

Calosi, C. & Wilson, J. M. (2022). Metaphysical indeterminacy in the multiverse. In V. Allori, ed., *Quantum Mechanics and Fundamentality: Naturalizing Quantum Theory between Scientific Realism and Ontological Indeterminacy*. Cham: Springer, pp. 375–395.

Cantor, G. (1878). Ein Beitrag zur Mannigfaltigkeitslehre. *Journal für die Reine und Angewandte Mathematik*, 1878(84), 242–258.

Casati, R. & Varzi, A. (1999). *Parts and Places*. Cambridge, MA: MIT Press.

Chen, E. K. (2022). Fundamental nomic vagueness. *Philosophical Review*, 131 (1), 1–49.

Cobreros, P., Egré, P., Ripley, D. & Rooij, R. (2013). Identity, Leibniz's Law and non-transitive reasoning. *Metaphysica*, 14(2), 253–264.

Cohen, P. J. (1963). The independence of the continuum hypothesis: Part I. *Proceedings of the National Academy of Sciences of the United States of America*, 50(6), 1143–1148.

Corti, A. (2021). Yet again, quantum indeterminacy is not worldly indecision. *Synthese*, 199(3), 5623–5643.

Cotnoir, A. J. & Varzi, A. C. (2021). *Mereology*. Oxford: Oxford University Press.

Dalla Chiara, M. L. & Giuntini, R. (2002). Quantum logics. In D. Gabbay & F. Guenthner, eds., *Handbook of Philosophical Logic*, 2nd ed., vol. 6. Dordrecht: Springer, pp. 129–228.

Darby, G. (2010). Quantum mechanics and metaphysical indeterminacy. *Australasian Journal of Philosophy*, 88(2), 227–245.

Darby, G. (2014). Vague objects in quantum mechanics? In K. Akiba & A. Abasnezhad, eds., *Vague Objects and Vague Identity: New Essays on Ontic Vagueness*. Dordrecht: Springer, pp. 69–108.

Darby, G. & Pickup, M. (2021). Modelling deep indeterminacy. *Synthese*, 198, 1685–1710.

Dorr, C. & Hawthorne, J. (2013). Naturalness. In K. Bennett & D. Zimmerman, eds., *Oxford Studies in Metaphysics*, vol. 8. Oxford: Oxford University Press, pp. 1–77.

Dummett, M. (1975). Wang's paradox. *Synthese*, 30(3–4), 201–232.

Einstein, A., Podolsky, B. & Rosen, N. (1935). Can quantum-mechanical description of physical reality be considered complete? *Physical Review*, 47 (10), 777–780.

Eklund, M. (2008). Deconstructing ontological vagueness. *Canadian Journal of Philosophy*, 38(1), 117–140.

Eklund, M. (2011). Being metaphysically unsettled: Barnes and Williams on metaphysical indeterminacy and vagueness. In K. Bennett & D. W. Zimmerman, eds., *Oxford Studies in Metaphysics*, vol. 6. Oxford: Oxford University Press, pp. 149–172.

Evans, G. (1978). Can there be vague objects? *Analysis*, 38(4), 208.

Fine, K. (1975). Vagueness, truth and logic. *Synthese*, 30(3–4), 265–300.

Fine, K. (2017). Truthmaker semantics. In C. Wright & B. Hale, eds., *A Companion to the Philosophy of Language*. Oxford: Blackwell, pp. 556–577.

Finocchiaro, P. (2019). Ideology and its role in metaphysics. *Synthese*, 198(2), 957–983.

Fletcher, S. C. & Taylor, D. E. (2021a). Quantum indeterminacy and the eigenstate-eigenvalue link. *Synthese*, 199(3–4), 1–32.

Fletcher, S. C. & Taylor, D. E. (2021b). Two quantum logics of indeterminacy. *Synthese*, 199(5–6), 13247–13281.

Frege, G. (1903). *Grundgesetze der Arithmetik, begriffsschriftlich abgeleitet*, vol. 2. Jena: Hermann Pohle.

French, S. & Krause, D. (2006). *Identity in Physics: A Historical, Philosophical, and Formal Analysis*. Oxford: Oxford University Press.

Gibbard, A. (1975). Contingent identity. *Journal of Philosophical Logic*, 4(2), 187–221.

Gilton, M. J. R. (2016). Whence the eigenstate-eigenvalue link? *Studies in History and Philosophy of Science Part B: Studies in History and Philosophy of Modern Physics*, 55, 92–100.

Glick, D. (2017). Against quantum indeterminacy. *Thought: A Journal of Philosophy*, 6(3), 204–213.

Glick, D. & Boge, F. J. (2021). Is the reality criterion analytic? *Erkenntnis*, 86 (6), 1445–1451.

Gödel, K. (1940). *The Consistency of the Continuum-Hypothesis*. Princeton, NJ: Princeton University Press.

Gómez Sánchez, V. (2022). Naturalness by law. Noûs 57 (1):100–127.

Hamkins, J. D. (2012). The set-theoretic multiverse. *Review of Symbolic Logic*, 5(3), 416–449.

Heller, M. (1996). Against metaphysical vagueness. *Philosophical Perspectives*, 10, 177–185.

Hempel, C. G. (1953). Reflections on Nelson Goodman's *The Structure of Appearance'. Philosophical Review*, 62, 108–116.

Keefe, R. (2000). *Theories of Vagueness*. Cambridge: Cambridge University Press.

Kleene, S. C. (1952). *Introduction to Metamathematics*. Princeton, NJ: North Holland.

Kochen, S. & Specker, E. (1967). The problem of hidden variables in quantum mechanics. *Journal of Mathematics and Mechanics*, 17, 59–87.

Ladyman, J. & Ross, D. (2007). *Every Thing Must Go: Metaphysics Naturalized*. Oxford: Oxford University Press.

Lewis, D. K. (1968). Counterpart theory and quantified modal logic. *Journal of Philosophy*, 65(5), 113–126.

Lewis, D. K. (1983). New work for a theory of universals. *Australasian Journal of Philosophy*, 61(4), 343–377.

Lewis, D. K. (1986). *On the Plurality of Worlds*. Oxford: Blackwell.

Lewis, D. K. (1988). Vague identity: Evans misunderstood. *Analysis*, 48(3), 128.

Lewis, D. K. (1991). *Parts of Classes*. Oxford: Blackwell.

Lewis, P. J. (2016). *Quantum Ontology: A Guide to the Metaphysics of Quantum Mechanics*. Oxford: Oxford University Press.

Lewis, P. J. (2022). Explicating quantum indeterminacy. In V. Allori, ed., *Quantum Mechanics and Fundamentality: Naturalizing Quantum Theory between Scientific Realism and Ontological Indeterminacy*. Cham: Springer, pp. 351–363.

Loss, R. (2018). Against "against 'against vague Existence.'" In K. Bennett & D. W. Zimmerman, eds., *Oxford Studies in Metaphysics*, vol. 11. Oxford: Oxford University Press, pp.278–288.

Lowe, E. J. (1994). Vague identity and quantum indeterminacy. *Analysis*, 54(2), 110–114.

Machina, K. F. (1976). Truth, belief, and vagueness. *Journal of Philosophical Logic*, 5(1), 47–78.

Mariani, C. (2021). Emergent quantum indeterminacy. *Ratio*, 34(3), 183–192.

Mariani, C. (2022a). Indeterminacy: Deep but not rock bottom. *Analytic Philosophy*, 63(1), 62–71.

Mariani, C. (2022b). Non-accessible mass and the ontology of GRW. *Studies in History and Philosophy of Science Part A*, 91, 270–279.

Mariani, C., Michels, R. & Torrengo, G. (2021). Plural metaphysical supervaluationism. *Inquiry: An Interdisciplinary Journal of Philosophy*, 1–38.

Mariani, C. & Torrengo, G. (2021). The indeterminate present and the open future. *Synthese*, 199(1–2), 3923–3944.

Maudlin, T. (2014). What Bell did. *Journal of Physics A: Mathematical and Theoretical*, 47(42), 424010.

McGee, V. & McLaughlin, B. (1994). Distinctions without a difference. *Southern Journal of Philosophy*, 33(S1), 203–251.

Merricks, T. (2001). Varieties of vagueness. *Philosophy and Phenomenological Research*, 62(1), 145–157.

Morreau, M. (2002). What vague objects are like. *Journal of Philosophy*, 99(7), 333–361.

Newhard, J. (2020). Alethic undecidability and alethic indeterminacy. *Synthese*, 199(1–2), 2563–2574.

Noonan, H. W. (1982). Vague objects. *Analysis*, 42(1), 3–6.

Parsons, J. (2007). Theories of location. In D. W. Zimmerman, ed., *Oxford Studies in Metaphysics*, vol. 3. Oxford: Oxford University Press, pp. 201–232.

Parsons, T. (2000). *Indeterminate Identity: Metaphysics and Semantics*. Oxford: Clarendon.

Quine, W. V. (1948). On what there is. *Review of Metaphysics*, 2(1), 21–38.

Rayo, A. (2017). The world is the totality of facts, not of things. *Philosophical Issues*, 27(1), 250–278.

Rayo, A. & Yablo, S. (2001). Nominalism through de-nominalization. *Noûs*, 35(1), 74–92.

Russell, B. (1923). Vagueness. *Australasian Journal of Philosophy*, 1(2), 84–92.

Scambler, C. (2020). An indeterminate univefse of sets. *Synthese*, 197(2), 545–573.

Schaffer, J. (2009). Spacetime the one substance. *Philosophical Studies*, 145(1), 131–148.

Schoenfield, M. (2016). Moral vagueness is ontic vagueness. *Ethics*, 126(2), 257–282.

Schroeren, D. (2021). Quantum metaphysical indeterminacy and the ontological foundations of orthodoxy. *Studies in History and Philosophy of Science Part A*, 90, 235–246.

Sider, T. (2011). *Writing the Book of the World*. Oxford: Oxford University Press.

Simons, P. (2004). Location. *Dialectica*, 58(3), 341–347.

Skow, B. (2010). Deep metaphysical indeterminacy. *Philosophical Quarterly*, 60(241), 851–858.

Smith, N. J. J. & Rosen, G. (2004). Worldly indeterminacy: A rough guide. *Australasian Journal of Philosophy*, 82(1), 185–198.

Sud, R. (forthcoming). Quantifier Variance, Vague Existence, and Metaphysical Vagueness. Journal of Philosophy.

Taylor, D. E. (2018). A minimal characterization of indeterminacy. *Philosophers' Imprint*, 18.

Taylor, D. E. & Burgess, A. (2015). What in the world is semantic indeterminacy? *Analytic Philosophy*, 56(4), 298–317.

Teller, P. (1986). Relational holism and quantum mechanics. *British Journal for the Philosophy of Science*, 37(1), 71–81.

Thomason, R. H. (1970). Indeterminist time and truth-value gaps. *Theoria*, 18 (3), 264–281.

Torza, A. (2020a). Quantum metaphysical indeterminacy and worldly incompleteness. *Synthese*, 197(10), 4251–4264.

Torza, A. (2020b). Structural indeterminacy. *Philosophy and Phenomenological Research*, 101(2), 365–382.

Torza, A. (2021). Quantum metametaphysics. *Synthese*, 199(3), 9809–9833.

Torza, A. (2022). Derivative metaphysical indeterminacy and quantum physics. In V. Allori, ed., *Quantum Mechanics and Fundamentality: Naturalizing Quantum Theory between Scientific Realism and Ontological Indeterminacy*. Cham: Springer, pp. 337–350.

Turner, J. (2016). *The Facts in Logical Space: A Tractarian Ontology*. Oxford: Oxford University Press.

Tye, M. (1994). Sorites paradoxes and the semantics of vagueness. *Philosophical Perspectives*, 8, 189–206.

Van Inwagen, P. (1987). When are objects parts? *Philosophical Perspectives*, 1, 21–47.

Van Inwagen, P. (1990). *Material Beings*. Ithaca, NY: Cornell University Press.

Von Neumann, J. (1955). *Mathematical Foundations of Quantum Mechanics*. Princeton, NJ: Princeton University Press.

Wallace, D. (2019). What is orthodox quantum mechanics? In A. Cordero, ed., *Philosophers Look at Quantum Mechanics*. Cham: Springer.

Wasserman, R. (2017). Vagueness and the laws of metaphysics. *Philosophy and Phenomenological Research*, 95(1), 66–89.

Weatherson, B. (2003). Many many problems. *Philosophical Quarterly*, 53 (213), 481–501.

Williams, J. R. G. (2008a). Multiple actualities and ontically vague identity. *Philosophical Quarterly*, 58(230), 134–154.

Williams, J. R. G. (2008b). Ontic vagueness and metaphysical indeterminacy. *Philosophy Compass*, 3(4), 763–788.

Williamson, T. (1994). *Vagueness*. London: Routledge.

Williamson, T. (1999). On the structure of higher-order Vagueness. *Mind*, 108 (429), 127–143.

Williamson, T. (2003a). Vagueness in reality. In M. J. Loux & D. W. Zimmerman, eds., *The Oxford Handbook of Metaphysics*. Oxford: Oxford University Press, pp. 690–715.

Williamson, T. (2003b). Everything. *Philosophical Perspectives*, 17(1), 415–465.

Williamson, T. (2013). *Modal logic as metaphysics*. Oxford University Press.

Wilson, Jessica M. (2017). Are There Indeterminate States of Affairs? Yes. In Elizabeth Barnes (ed.), Current Controversies in Metaphysics. Taylor & Francis. pp. 105–119.

Wilson, A. (2020). *The Nature of Contingency: Quantum Physics As Modal Realism*. Oxford: Oxford University Press.

Wilson, J. M. (2013). A determinable-based account of metaphysical indeterminacy. *Inquiry: An Interdisciplinary Journal of Philosophy*, 56(4), 359–385.

Wittgenstein, L. (1921). *Tractatus Logico-Philosophicus*. London: Routledge & Kegan Paul. Translated 1961 by D. F. Pears & B. F. McGuinness.

Wolff, J. (2015). Spin as a determinable. *Topoi*, 34(2), 379–386.

Acknowledgments

Many thanks to Ken Akiba, Claudio Calosi, David Taylor, and Jessica Wilson for their invaluable feedback on ideas that made it to this Element. I am also indebted to the Metaphysics Seminar of the Institute for Philosophical Research at UNAM, as well as two anonymous referees for reading and commenting on previous versions of the manuscript, and to the series editor Tuomas Tahko. Finally, I wish to thank my favorite six-legged creature for being there, and determinately so.

Cambridge Elements

Metaphysics

Tuomas E. Tahko
University of Bristol

Tuomas E. Tahko is Professor of Metaphysics of Science at the University of Bristol, UK. Tahko specializes in contemporary analytic metaphysics, with an emphasis on methodological and epistemic issues: 'meta-metaphysics'. He also works at the interface of metaphysics and philosophy of science: 'metaphysics of science'. Tahko is the author of *Unity of Science* (Cambridge University Press, 2021, *Elements in Philosophy of Science*), *An Introduction to Metametaphysics* (Cambridge University Press, 2015) and editor of *Contemporary Aristotelian Metaphysics* (Cambridge University Press, 2012).

About the Series

This highly accessible series of Elements provides brief but comprehensive introductions to the most central topics in metaphysics. Many of the Elements also go into considerable depth, so the series will appeal to both students and academics. Some Elements bridge the gaps between metaphysics, philosophy of science, and epistemology.

Cambridge Elements ☰

Metaphysics

Printed in the United States
by Baker & Taylor Publisher Services